Midwestern Miscellany

LII
Spring–Fall 2024

I0558691

Banned in the Heartland

Guest Editor
John Rohrkemper

The Midwestern Press

Copy Editing and Design
Patricia Oman

© 2024 The Society for the Study of Midwestern Literature

All rights reserved. No part of this work may be reproduced in
any form without permission of the publisher.

Midwestern Miscellany (ISSN 0885-4742) is a peer-reviewed journal published
twice a year (Spring and Fall) by the Society for the Study of Midwestern Literature.

The journal is a member of the Council of Editors of Learned Journals.

This special edition of *Midwestern Miscellany*,
"Banned in the Heartland,"
is dedicated to

MATTHEW GOOD

and all American librarians working for free
and unfettered access to knowledge and information

CONTENTS

PREFACE

John Rohrkemper

The desire to know, to learn about our world, to discover who we are and how we differ from others—and what we share with others, as well—is as old as humanity; it is likely that the desire to shut down such pursuits, to prevent others from knowing, is nearly as old. Today in America the battle over access to ideas, and specifically access to books, is waged in our statehouses and our schoolboard meetings, and plays out in our classrooms and our school libraries. The impulse to ban books and, on the other hand, to defend open access to them, is a volatile front in our culture wars.

This collection of essays addresses this conflict, though it is fair to say that the authors of these pieces are hardly neutral observers. As custodians of our culture, we have a stake in keeping all means of inquiry open. All the authors here are partisans, committed to the book and its liberating power. Our contributors show us that the struggle over books, over ideas, is not a new phenomenon in American or specifically midwestern culture. The first three essays consider battles over what we now generally consider canonical books from the early twentieth century. The other four essays examine how the controversy over books plays out a century later, in our time.

There are, it would seem, different motives for wanting to ban certain works. First, governments and other seats of authority sometimes want to limit access to knowledge to maintain a firm control over which ideas are deemed acceptable in society. Knowledge is a prerequisite for freedom in the world of ideas. Control access to knowledge, so the thinking seems to go, and one can dictate what may be considered truth. And so, dictators confiscate and burn books and elected officials try to remove them from our curricula and pluck them from the shelves of our school libraries. But such top-down, hierarchical censorship is not all of it. The urge to censor also bubbles up from below in populist movements that seem to fear the dawning future enough to try to deny it by banning the books that seem to point the way to that tomorrow. Of course, these top-down and bottom-up phenomena are often symbiotic, feeding on and exploiting the other. A third impulse might come from a different ideological direction: a desire to ignore an imperfect past in which characters may have spoken in ways we today find vulgar or demeaning, acted in ways we deem despicable.

Two events inspired me to propose this special issue of the *Miscellany*. One was the accidentally simultaneous reading of two books about book banning, both by midwestern authors: Ray Bradbury's *Fahrenheit 451* and Celeste Ng's *Our Missing Hearts*. Both are set in dystopian societies that may be futuristic but feel unsettlingly like today. Both are dark and disturbing views, but Ng's 2022 novel embraces hope in a band of heroes working to subvert the authoritarian regime and its war on ideas. The unlikely heroes of *Our Missing Hearts* are librarians who risk their careers and possibly their own personal liberty by forming a virtual Underground Railroad, protecting and transporting suspect people and books. The second event that inspired me was the November 2022 decision by my friend Matthew Good to resign his long-held position as a school librarian in Lancaster County, Pennsylvania, because he believed it a violation of his vocation's ethics to keep books *from* his students as his school district increasingly was demanding. Good, a Holocaust educator as well as a librarian, knew too well the consequences of censorship. With that difficult decision, a friend became to me a hero.

Elizabethtown College

BANNED IN LEWISTON

Edgar Lee Masters's *Spoon River Anthology*

Marcia Noe

Rape! Prostitution! Adultery! Murder! Abortion! Suicide! Is it any wonder that the citizens of Lewiston, Illinois, were concerned when Edgar Lee Masters, who grew up in that town, published a book of poems called *Spoon River Anthology* that dealt with those very topics. There was little doubt that Lewiston, where the Spoon River flowed near the edge of town, was the setting for Masters's book, which comprises 244 dramatic monologues in free verse spoken by the residents of the municipal cemetery who relate their troubled pasts, reveal their neighbors' secret lives, and expose corruption in the local power structure. "Spoon River is essentially a picture of a society maimed by puritanism, materialism, narrow religion and hypocrisy," asserts Ernest Earnest (63).

Lewiston residents may have been especially concerned because of the book's notoriety. *Spoon River Anthology* was not an obscure collection of verses that would languish on library shelves; it was a publishing sensation that would become an international best seller and be widely reviewed, translated into several languages, and published in more than seventy editions. It has never been out of print in over one hundred years (Hartley, *Spoon River Revisited* 24). However, despite the book's success, it was banned from Lewiston public schools and the Lewiston Carnegie Library, where Masters's mother, Emma Jerusha Dexter Masters, had served as vice-president of the first library board. This ban was not lifted until 1974 (Scanlan 7). Although *Spoon River Anthology* did include poems about sex and crime, as well as negative poems about easily identifiable Lewiston individuals, the real impetus for the ban appears to be the book's radical departure from conventional morals and mores, its deviation from the genteel literary tradition, and, especially, its liberal political orientation. When viewed in light of the current spate of book-banning and censorship, *Spoon River Anthology* takes on a new significance for its ability to build connections and encourage empathy among its readers.

Ironically, Masters did not compose the poems in Lewiston but in Chicago, whence he had fled after an unhappy stint in his father's law office. There a number of factors converged to produce *Spoon River Anthology*. There in Chicago his friend William Marion Reedy introduced him to the *Greek Anthology*, which sparked Masters's imagination. There, too, a visit from Masters's mother in May of 1914 further inspired him as the two talked over the old times of his boyhood in Lewiston and Petersburg, Illinois. And there Masters was able to connect with writers of the Chicago Renaissance such as Carl Sandburg, Theodore Dreiser, Harriet Monroe, Eunice Tietjens, Arthur Davison Ficke and Floyd Dell.[1] Sustained and stimulated by this supportive literary community, he composed the *Spoon River* poems over an eight-month period in 1914, sending them to Reedy in St. Louis, who published them in his literary magazine, the *Mirror*, between May 29, 1914, and January 15, 1915. The forty-five-year-old lawyer/poet continued to add verses to make an anthology, and the Macmillan Company in New York City published them in book form on April 15, 1915 (Hurt 407–09).[2]

Unlike Masters's Lewiston family, friends, and neighbors, most critics responded positively to *Spoon River Anthology*. While some objected to the sordid situations and harsh language of the book, and others wondered whether it was really poetry, many recognized it as a ground-breaking literary work, comparing Masters to Robert Frost and Edward Arlington Robinson, as well as Dante, Shakespeare, and Balzac. "It is the first successful novel in verse we have had in American literature," noted William Stanley Braithwaite in the *Boston Evening Transcript*.[3]

"Surely Mr. Masters has written great stuff," enthused Nathan Haskell Doyle (N. H. D.). Floyd Dell agreed, opining that "we are likely to find a strange impressiveness akin to greatness in the 'Spoon River Anthology' of Edgar Lee Masters" (14). One critic in the *American Review of Reviews* called the book "a highly successful and unique addition to American poetry," and Lawrence Gilman lauded Masters for creating a new art form, "the cinematographing of narrative prose" ("Poetry, American and Foreign" 758; Gilman 274). Alice Corbin Henderson discussed Masters's achievement within an international context: "[H]e has given an intensely vital meaning to our immediate human environment. He has done for us what the young

Irish writers have done for Ireland" (A. C. H. 149). "There has, indeed, been some excellent philosophy garnered on the banks of Spoon River for him who cares to profit by it" concluded the reviewer for *The New York Times* ("A Human Anthology" 261).

If a classic is a book that has legs or children, *Spoon River Anthology* easily qualifies. Singled out by Carl Van Doren in his landmark essay in the *Nation* as the book that ignited the revolt from the village literary movement, *Spoon River Anthology* influenced Sherwood Anderson's *Winesburg, Ohio* (1919) and Sinclair Lewis's *Main Street* (1920) and has generated more than fifty scholarly articles and books (407, 408, 410). "*Spoon River Anthology* has been read, performed, praised, attacked, debated, even censored for over sixty-five years," noted Ronald Primeau in 1981 (Preface x).

Indeed, *Spoon River Anthology* has lived on as an intertext of works of music, fiction, drama, and poetry throughout the twentieth century and into the twenty-first. In Thornton Wilder's play *Our Town* (1938), the last act is set in the town cemetery with the dead speaking from their graves. The playwright acknowledged his debt to Masters by misquoting (possibly on purpose) "Lucinda Matlock": "It's like one of those Middle West poets said: You've got to love life to have life, and you've got to have life to love life" (49).[4]

In *Spoon River America* (2021) historian Jason Stacy cites the CBS Radio Workshop play *Epitaphs* (1957) and Charles Aidman's musical adaptation for Broadway (1963), as well as Melvin B. Tolson's *A Gallery of Harlem Portraits* (1980), as intertexts of *Spoon River Anthology* and notes that the book is frequently taught in secondary school English classes, with students often assigned to write their own dramatic monologues in *Spoon River* fashion. Dave Etter's *Alliance, Illinois* (1983) is a late twentieth-century revision of Masters's classic, and George Saunders's first novel, *Lincoln in the Bardo* (2017), which *The New York Times* critic Michiko Kakutani likens to *Spoon River Anthology*, brings Masters into the twenty-first, with Kakutani pointing out that the book "appropriates Masters's multivoiced approach, using it to create a story that unfolds into a meditation on the dramas and disappointments of ordinary people, longing for connection but often left feeling isolated and alone" (C1, C3).[5]

Present-day scholars and critics also admire the book and acknowledge its impact. John E. Hallwas, who edited and introduced an annotated edition of *Spoon River Anthology*, points out that "[n]o volume of poetry since Whitman's *Leaves of Grass* (1855) had attempted so much or had been so original" (Introduction 1). Masters's biographer, Herbert K. Russell, says that the book "yielded a literary and social uproar unlike that of any other book of American poetry published before or after" (56). And Earnest contends that "no other volume of poetry except *The Waste Land* (1922) made such an impact during the first quarter of this century" (59).

In light of these accolades, one might wonder why the good people of Lewiston weren't more appreciative of *Spoon River Anthology*. Some elite and middle-class Lewiston readers might have found the book objectionable because it was just not the kind of writing they knew as poetry. By 1915, modernism as a literary movement was well underway; T. S. Eliot published "The Love Song of J. Alfred Prufrock" in *Poetry* in 1915, and Carl Sandburg and James Joyce published *Chicago Poems* and *A Portrait of the Artist as a Young Man* respectively the following year. However, the genteel literary tradition still held sway, especially in towns and villages far from literary centers such as Boston, Chicago, London, Paris, and New York City. For such readers, poetry was something that rhymed and scanned and centered on lofty subjects and heroic people, like Henry Wadsworth Longfellow's poems about Paul Revere and Hiawatha. Above all, they expected poetry to edify them and help them to become better people, as Longfellow in "Psalm of Life" aspired to do.

Such readers may have balked at *Spoon River* monologues such as those spoken by sex worker Daisy Fraser, rape victim Minerva Jones, suicide Julia Miller, arsonist Nancy Knapp, abortionist Doctor Meyers, murderer Barry Holden, and fornicators Reuben Pantier and Dora Miller. Moreover, they may have found graphic descriptions like that found in Indignation Jones's lament a bit hard to take: "Sometimes a man's life turns into a cancer / From being bruised and continually bruised, / And swells into a purplish mass, / Like growths on stalks of corn" (109). The *Spoon River* poems were, to these readers, a shocking departure from literary tradition.

Robert Narveson calls them "poetry of a comparatively classless democratic society" (62). William Dean Howells calls them "shredded prose" (635).

Taken as a whole, the *Spoon River* poems question widely held middle-class conventions, such as patriotism and monogamy, and critique the political and social structures that enforce them, a thematic emphasis not likely to please the Lewiston reading public. Charles E. Burgess points out that even Mary Fisher, one of Masters's high school teachers and an intellectual influence, held "a stiffly conventional view of morals and manners" that he critiqued throughout the book ("Masters" 186). Such a critique is evident in "Knowlt Hoheimer," who died at Missionary Ridge during the Civil War and resents the words carved on his granite monument: "Pro Patria." The last line of the poem is, "What do they mean, anyway?" (113).

Lewiston citizens also may have resented Masters's washing the town's dirty linen in *Spoon River*. Masters himself pointed out that the poems in the first part of the book, based on his teen years in Lewiston, tended to be more negative than those in the second half that were inspired by his idyllic experience on his paternal grandparents' farm near Petersburg. He characterized the former poems as depicting fools, drunkards, failures, and people of one-birth minds and the latter as portraying heroes and enlightened spirits ("Genesis" 50). And then there were the people who took it personally, some with good reason. Masters readily admitted that he had based a number of the poems on actual Lewiston- and Petersburg-area residents, past and present. He changed some of the names very little and a very few not at all, no doubt adding fuel to their ire. In an article for *American Mercury*, Masters even got specific, stating that fifty-three poems featured names from Petersburg and its environs while sixty-six used names from the Lewiston area. "In a word, no town of 3,500 people ever had more curious, colorful characters than this one," asserted Masters of Lewiston. "I knew them all" ("Genesis" 40–41).

That he did was glaringly apparent in many of the Lewiston-based poems. In "Chase Henry," Masters barely altered the name of Frank "Chase" Henry, the town drunk who burned down the Lewiston courthouse (Hallwas, Notes 368). "Lucius Atherton" was inspired by Lewis C. (Lute) Ross; the poem depicts an elderly womanizer no longer attractive enough to seduce young girls: "a gray, untidy, / Tooth-less, discarded, rural Don Juan …" (142, ellipses in original). "Henry Phipps" was based on Henry Phelps, a Lewiston businessman with strong ties to what Masters called "the courthouse ring" (Hallwas, Notes 417). "Benjamin Pantier" and "Mrs. Benjamin Pantier" reflect the sorry state of Masters's parents' marriage, as well as that of his own. Benjamin is buried with his dog, blaming "she, who survives me, snared my soul / With a snare which bled me to death, / Till I, once strong of will, lay broken, indifferent" (101). Of course, Mrs. Pantier has her own side of the story: "But suppose you are really a lady, and have delicate tastes, / And loathe the smell of whiskey and onions … And the only man with whom the law and morality / Permit you to have the marital relation / Is the very man that fills you with disgust …" (102).

"Editor Whedon" is a thinly disguised portrait of William Taylor Davidson, editor of the Fulton *Democrat*, "who accepted bribes for political support and then betrayed his bargains" (Masters, "Genesis" 42). In this poem and throughout the book, Masters weaves motifs of disease, toxicity, and decay to suggest moral de-terioration: "Poisoned with the anonymous words / Of your clandestine soul … Then to lie here close by the river over the place / Where the sewage flows from the village, / And the empty cans and garbage are dumped, / And abortions are hidden" (213).[6]

Davidson's wife, Margaret Gilman George Davidson, who was one of Mas-ters's close friends in Lewiston, was thought to be the model for "Julia Miller"; Masters himself asserts that he "employed the aura of her personality" in "Caroline Branson," and "Amelia Garrick" ("Genesis" 45). Burgess states that "[d]escendants of the Davidson family were outraged when Masters introduced into *Spoon River* some unmistakable facts and imaginative implications about Margaret's marriage and death" ("Masters" 191).

At the center of Spoon River's web of corruption sits banker Thomas Rhodes, a nefarious spider spinning out strands of control to ensnare and destroy Spoon River citizens like cashier George Reece, who was framed, convicted, and incarcer-ated for the failure of Rhodes's bank. This corrupt network comprises Thomas and

Ralph Rhodes, the banker's son; Mayor A. D. Blood; editor Coolbaugh Whedon; the Reverend Abner Peet; Justice Somers; lobbyist Elliott Hawkins; land dealer Christian Dallman; industrialist Lambert Hutchins; the Town Marshall; and Henry Phipps, banker and Sunday School superintendent, who was the titular president of the canning factory and the wagon works but was really the puppet of Rhodes and his cronies (Burgess, "Spoon River" 353).[7]

Rhodes, like Phipps, was modeled on Henry Phelps, who, Masters contends, "deserved all that I said about him" ("Genesis" 50).[8] Phelps was one of the main power brokers in Lewistown, a partner in the mercantile firm of Phelps and Proctor and chief officer of a failing bank who had served as president of the village council and superintendent of the Presbyterian Church's Sunday School (Burgess, "Spoon River" 354). Hallwas calls Thomas Rhodes "the arch-villain in *Spoon River Anthology*" and observes that Rhodes is mentioned in twenty of the *Spoon River* poems (Notes 394). In his short monologue, Rhodes mocks liberals, intellectuals, and artists: "You found with all your boasted wisdom / How hard at the last it is / To keep the soul from splitting into cellular atoms" (191).[9]

And as if exposing the town's sins and sinners weren't bad enough, *Spoon River Anthology*'s politics must have been too big a live toad for conservative Lewiston residents to swallow. Like his father, Masters was a lifelong Democrat who supported the free coinage of silver, opposed the American imperialist war in the Philippines, and blamed industrial capitalism for the pernicious social changes that were decimating America's towns and villages and blighting her cities (Hartley, "Edgar Lee Masters" 253–55). As Earnest points out, he wrote from "the Jeffersonian tradition of free inquiry, humanitarianism, egalitarianism," a tradition reflected in many of the *Spoon River* monologues that was incompatible with the prevailing politics of the town (61).

Masters's liberal proclivities are readily in evidence in an earlier book, *The New Star Chamber* (1904), the title essay of which likens the anti-labor chancery court to the English courts that wielded tyrannical power from 1487 to 1641. Here Masters portrays the judiciary of his day as little more than an arm of corporate America that routinely enjoined labor unions from striking. Ironically, these injunctions were issued under the guise of liberty; supposedly, they protected the employer's freedom to hire whom he chose and the workingman's freedom to work without constraint. In actuality, Masters argues, what the chancery court prevents with its injunctions is competition, relieving the employer from paying workers the competitive wages that would have been gained from a strike and enabling him to pay the lower wages that prevailed because workers were unable to strike. "Usurpation and hypocrisy have never been more thinly veiled," scolded Masters (*New Star Chamber* 29). Ronald Primeau comments that Masters was "first and foremost a populist who saw great hope for the democratic experiment if matters were left to people rather than being squashed by the rich and powerful with their misuse of institutions" (Afterword 296).

Moreover, Masters no doubt angered the Law and Order Party in Lewiston with the poems that lionize John Peter Altgeld, the Illinois governor who pardoned three of the activists convicted for the 1886 Haymarket Square violence. He portrays "Carl Hamblin," the liberal newspaper editor, as having been tarred and feathered for publishing a sympathetic poem on the day that the Haymarket activists were hanged; the poem portrays Justice with bandaged, diseased eyes, striking out with a sword: "Sometimes striking a child / Again a laborer / Again a slinking woman, again a lunatic" (212). In "Magrady Graham," Altgeld is described as having "an air of eternity about him, / Like the cold, clear light that rests at dawn / On the hills!" (266). Narveson suggests that "Herman Altman" was a pseudonymous portrait of Altgeld, "who could not with plausibility be smuggled into the Spoon River graveyard under his own name" (60). "Did I follow Truth wherever she led, / And stand against the whole world for a cause, / And uphold the weak against the strong?" asks Altman rhetorically (297).

As a Chicago attorney whose law partner was Clarence Darrow, Masters often took pro bono cases in which he argued for the underdog. While writing the *Spoon River* poems, he was representing the Waitresses' Union in an injunction case (Masters, *Across Spoon River* 334). This pro-labor stance is reflected in the *Spoon River* poems, a number of which emphasize how few legal protections workers had during the World War I years. At a time before Workmen's Compensation, "Butch

Weldy" relates the story of a man who was blinded and maimed by an explosion at Thomas Rhodes's canning factory but was unable to recover damages from his employer. "Such attempts were often stymied by the corruption of the court system, which served factory owners at the expense of the working class, as industrial wealth made bribery common and legal protection of corporate monopolistic practices virtually unassailable," notes Stacy (Introduction 7).

A number of the *Spoon River* poems focus on this kind of injustice. "John M. Church," an insurance lawyer who worked for the railroad, relates how he fixed the judge and jury "to beat the claims / Of the crippled, the widow and orphan, / And made a fortune thereat" (169). "John Hancock Otis" complains that a Spoon River citizen of humble background became superintendent of the railroad and was "a veritable slave driver, / Grinding the faces of labor, / And a bitter enemy of democracy" (205). "When the people clamor for freedom / They really seek for power o'er the strong," responds "Anthony Findlay" (206). Stacy asserts that "the epitaphs of Spoon River exhibit the unmistakable fingerprints of Masters's anti-imperialism, anti-elitism, and Populist sympathies" (*New Star Chamber* 11). K. Narayanda Chandran agrees that the poems enact this kind of social critique: "Spoon River … betrays its age-old commitment to the agrarian cause, violates its traditional faith in the therapeutic virtues of country life …" (444). For Herbert Ellsworth Childs, too, they express Masters's disappointment that Jeffersonian agrarianism was waning in rural America and taking with it the "simple neighborly virtues" it engendered, such as honesty, integrity, and neighborliness. "Spoon River represents to Mr. Masters a failure in social justice," concludes Childs (337, 334).

Reading *Spoon River Anthology* in light of today's censorship controversies is an exercise in poignant nostalgia. The poems, for the most part, are innocent of the current hot button issues that have sparked so much activism targeting teachers and librarians: race, gender, sexuality, and LGBTQ+ topics. Only 38 of the 244 poems deal with sex, and none explicitly describes a sex act (Earnest 63). The liberal orientation of the book might be a problem for today's conservative readers, but they would have to read all 244 poems and piece together Masters's political philosophy from their allusions and patterns, as well as develop an informed understanding of the political issues that obtained in his day, to be able to understand his politics with complete comprehension.

Moreover, *Spoon River Anthology* was written for adults, while the censorship spotlight today has shifted to books for young readers. John Green, author of *Looking for Alaska* (2005) and *The Fault in Our Stars* (2012), says he has been faced with efforts to censor his books for about as long as he has been publishing them but is now dealing with an even more unhappy circumstance: the East Hamilton library in his home state of Indiana has adopted a policy of shelving books with sexually explicit content in the adult section of the library. Similar policies have been implemented in Montgomery County, Texas; Campbell County, Wyoming; Crawford County, Arkansas; and Marion County, Mississippi. "I believe very strongly in the freedom of expression and in teenagers' rights to read, and I feel very strongly that other parents shouldn't have any say in what my kids get to read," Green stated. "As long as that fight goes on, I feel obligated to lend my voice to it" (Alter).

And that fight, assuredly, will go on. Perhaps the most extreme measure was that passed by the Iowa State Legislature in the spring of 2023. This law holds public education officials directly responsible if the school library includes any books containing depictions of sex acts. Lacking guidance from the Iowa Department of Education on how to implement this policy, one school system administrator turned to ChatGPT and incurred the Internet-fueled wrath of the likes of the American Civil Liberties Union and *Rolling Stone*. "I believe in parents' rights. I want all the parents in our country to be actively making the decisions they believe are best for their children," said Bridgette Exman, Assistant Superintendent of Curriculum and Instruction for public schools in Mason City, Iowa. "At the same time, let's not overlook our collective responsibility to achieve the goal of the American public education system—to ensure that every child has access to the highest quality teaching and opportunities for learning" (Exman).

In the summer of 2023, the state of Texas brought the censorship battle to bookstores, requiring them to establish a rating system based on sexual content for titles that they sell to schools; those that fail to do so will be prohibited from doing business with them. Booksellers in Houston and Austin have brought suit on First

Amendment grounds, supported by the American Booksellers Association, the Association of American Publishers, the Authors Guild, and the Comic Book Legal Defense Fund. The new law has already restricted access before it has even taken effect; the Katy Independent School District outside Houston is no longer buying books and has put all of the books they now hold into storage until they can be rated (Alter and Harris).

In some states censorship starts at the top. Novelist Carl Hiaasen writes that Governor Ron DeSantis "has succeeded in stifling discussions of gender identity and Black history in public education. Books are now being yanked from Florida school libraries and classrooms for review if just one person complains ... Novels by a span of authors from Judy Blume to Aldous Huxley to Toni Morrison (and, full disclosure, myself) have been pulled from school shelves. A Miami Lakes pre-K-through-eighth-grade school actually flagged 'The Hill We Climb,' Amanda Gorman's best-selling inauguration poem, as inappropriate for younger children after a parent claimed to have deciphered 'hate messages' in the verses" (41).

Policies like these, of course, amount to book banning and censorship if they deny access to the books' intended audience—in these cases, student readers. Irene Mulvey, President of the American Association of University Professors, points out that such policies violate the First Amendment to the US Constitution. Writing in AAUP's semi-annual journal, *Academe,* Mulvey warns that attacks on libraries are attacks on our democracy. "A healthy democracy requires an informed and engaged populace. The freedoms guaranteed by the First Amendment are fully realized only when people have unfettered access to uncensored information as well as high-quality and affordable public education" (56). Masters himself spoke to this point when he said that he wrote *Spoon River Anthology* "to awaken that American vision, that love of liberty which the best men of the Republic strove to win for us, and to bequeath to time" ("Genesis" 55).

In 1943, the Defense Department recognized the role of reading, literacy, and literature in preserving democracy when they issued the Armed Services Editions, a series of pocket-sized paperback books for soldiers serving in World War II that included Herman Melville's *Typee* and F. Scott Fitzgerald's *The Great Gatsby,* as well as more contemporary titles. "Books were seen not just as diversions, but as weapons in the fight for democracy," asserts Jennifer Schuessler (C6). The program's wide distribution of more than 1,300 titles created a postwar demand for paperback books that helped to expand America's reading public, especially among the young men who had first encountered one of these books during wartime. Schuessler points out that this program helped *The Great Gatsby* achieve canonical status after more than 120,000 copies of the Armed Services Edition of this novel were distributed (C6).

Today the censorship picture in America looks grim. In March of 2023, the American Library Association (ALA) issued a report that documented nearly 1,300 book-banning attempts in the United States during the previous year, the largest number since the Association began compiling such statistics. (Alter, Cruz, and Harris). The most recent ALA report shows that nearly 50% of the book complaints lodged during the first half of 2023 were issued in public libraries, and that most of the books in question were by or about people of color or LGBTQ people. "A year and a half ago, we were told that these books didn't belong in school libraries, and if people wanted to read them, they could go to a public library," remarked Deborah Caldwell-Stone, Director of the ALA's Office for Intellectual Freedom. PEN America, a writers' association, reported 3,362 cases of book removals from school and classroom libraries during the 2022–23 academic year, a 33% increase over the previous year (Harris and Alter).

But a hopeful development occurred, interestingly enough, in Masters's home state of Illinois, when the legislature passed the first law in the country that prohibits book-banning. Signing the bill into law on June 12, 2023, Governor J. B. Pritzker became a leading warrior in the fight for First Amendment rights: "Book bans are about censorship, marginalizing people, marginalizing ideas and facts," he stated. "Regimes ban books, not democracies ("Illinois Becomes").

One regime that bans books is the one currently in power in the Islamic Republic of Iran. In *Reading Lolita in Tehran*, Azar Nafisi relates how, in order to read and discuss classics by Nabokov, Fitzgerald, James, and Austen, she was forced by state censorship to convene a clandestine reading group in her home in a room that became "a place of transgression" (8). "I have a recurring fantasy that one more article has been added to the Bill of Rights," Nafisi wrote in her notebook in June of 1997, "the right to free access to imagination. I have come to believe that genuine democracy cannot exist without the freedom to imagine and the right to use imaginative works without any restrictions" (338–39). Primeau concurs with this view, noting that, once again with freedom of speech under attack, Masters is raising a voice of resistance, critique, subversion, and empowerment in *Spoon River Anthology* that makes it as compelling today as it was in 1915.

It's worth exploring at greater length why Masters, Pritzker, Mulvey, Nafisi, and Primeau, among many others, have been so vigilant against book banning and censorship. Our First Amendment rights that such actions violate are, of course, vital in preserving American democracy, as discussed above. Another salient issue is that books, literature, and reading are of compelling public interest because they are social goods benefiting both individuals and society. In the 1960s, Mary S. Snouffer and Patricia Rinehart reported success in teaching some poems from *Spoon River Anthology* to working-class students who had had little previous exposure to poetry. They found that the poems encouraged students to identify "the counterparts in real life, selecting national as well as local figures." One of their students subsequently made a request: "I would like to hear some more of *them* poems about people" (46, italics in original).

This student's request offers insight into *Spoon River Anthology*'s longevity and significance. Primeau elaborates on this point, making a strong case for the book's continuing relevance: "Masters discovered a voice that spoke to and for a public that made the work popular because it expressed what they felt and believed but could not express for themselves." He also demonstrates its contemporary significance in terms of form: "Masters shaped structures that would be comfortably at home in a world of e-mail exchanges, list serve flowing of data [sic], search engines that go nearly everywhere, hypertexts that make us participants, and new patterns resulting from the digitalization of video and film" (Afterword 296, 298).

The student's comment also alludes to literature's power to involve readers in many varied experiences, cultures, and realities. In *The Whalebone Theatre*, novelist Joanna Quinn emphasizes this point, writing of children whose treasured possessions were *Alice's Adventures in Wonderland, Tales from Shakespeare,* and other books, "Their most-loved books have been read so many times, they only have to look at the covers to know how it feels to be enclosed within them. But the worlds contained within the books do not remain between the covers. They seep out and overlay the geography of their lives" (125).

Reading widely helps us understand that people everywhere are similar. Masters achieved this insight when he realized that everything that was true of Spoon River was also true of Chicago: "I came to the conclusion that the city banker was no other than the country banker, the city lawyer the same as the country lawyer, the city preacher the same as the country preacher, and the theology, finance, jurisprudence, society, and the antitheses of good and evil the same in both the city and the country towns. The village of Lewistown had furnished me a key which unlocked the secrets of the world at large" ("Genesis" 46).

And while reading does make us aware of our commonalities, of the things that we share as humans, at the same time, it also introduces us to people of different genders, races, religions, sexual orientations, ethnicities, social classes, cultures, and nations, and, in so doing, provides additional perspectives that can modify our opinions and feelings. "Imagining the other is a powerful antidote to fanaticism and hatred," notes Israeli author Amos Oz (Balint). Studies done at the University of Iowa and at the New School show that reading fiction makes people more empathetic, findings that support Oz's opinion (Chiaet). Another advocate for reading as a social good that builds connections among people is Pulitzer Prize–winning playwright Susan Glaspell, who argues that "the best books take us a little farther into understanding, into tolerance, to a keener amusement, and to warmer sympathies" (1–2).

And while the dangers of book banning, book burning, book suppression, neglected literature, forgotten literature, and censorship recur throughout the pages of *Spoon River Anthology,* in "Jeremy Carlisle" Masters, like Oz and Glaspell, reminds us of reading's power to engender empathy: "Passerby, sin beyond any sin / Is the sin of blindness of souls to other souls. / And joy beyond any joy is the joy / Of having the good in you seen and seeing the good / At the miraculous moment!" (325).[10] Thanks to the heroic efforts of First Amendment activists like those described above, we will continue to be able to read *Spoon River Anthology*, as well as other works of literature, that can enrich our lives, expand our perspectives, and enhance our capacity for empathy, something that we Americans could use a whole lot more of these days.

University of Tennessee at Chattanooga

Notes

1. Monroe and Tietjens were editors of *Poetry: A Magazine of Verse*, founded in Chicago in 1912. The first issue of *Poetry* featured a poem by Ficke, then living in Davenport, Iowa, who made periodic trips to Chicago to socialize at Floyd Dell and wife Margery Currey's salon. Dell, another Davenporter, moved to Chicago in 1908; a few years later, he became editor of the *Friday Literary Review* of the *Chicago Evening Post.* His second novel, *The Briary-Bush* (1921), is set in Chicago. Dreiser was a Terre Haute, Indiana, native; his novels *Sister Carrie* (1900), *Jennie Gerhard* (1911), *The Financier* (1912), *The Titan* (1914), and *The Stoic* (1947) are set in Chicago. Sandburg, from Galesburg, Illinois, moved to Chicago in 1912, where he worked as a journalist and wrote poetry. He won *Poetry*'s Helen Haire Levenson Prize in 1914 and published *Chicago Poems* in 1916.

2. *Spoon River Anthology* was not Masters's first book. He had actually published several earlier volumes, none of which did very well in terms of critical or popular reception: *A Book of Verses* (1898), *Maximilian: A Play in Five Acts* (1902), *The New Star Chamber and Other Essays* (1904), *Althea: A Play in Four Acts* (1907), *The Trifler: A Play* (1908), *The Blood of the Prophets* (1909), *The Leaves of the Tree: A Play* (1909), *Eileen: A Play in Three Acts* (1910), *Songs and Sonnets* [Webster Ford] (1910), *The Locket: A Play in Three Acts* (1910), *The Bread of Idleness: A Play in Four Acts* (1911), *Songs and Sonnets: Second Series* [Webster Ford] (1912), and *Browning as a Philosopher* (1912).

3. See Flanagan for a comprehensive annotated bibliography of the contemporaneous critical response to *Spoon River Anthology* and other works by Masters, as well as a brief account of the poet's life.

4. The last line of "Lucinda Matlock," a poem based on Masters's paternal grandmother, Lucinda Young Masters, is, "It takes life to love Life" (295).

5. *Spoon River Anthology*'s wide appeal has persisted through the decades to the present day, inspiring many adaptations and works in other genres. CBS produced a television adaptation on April 21, 1969, that starred Jason Robards, Jr., Charles Aidman, Joyce Van Patten, and Jennifer West (Burgess, "Local Lore" 157n4). In 2005 the Creative Learning Lab at Utah State University developed a game, *Voices of Spoon River*, and in March of 2021, the Oxford University Dramatic Society performed an online reading, "Anthology of Spoon River." The book was especially well received in Italy: in 1971, Fabrizio De Andre recorded a concept album inspired by *Spoon River Anthology*, *Non al denaro non all'amore ne al cielo*; in 1974, photographer Mario Giaomelli created "Homage to Spoon River," a series of abstract photographs; and in 2015, Nene Grignaffini and Francesco Conversano debuted their film, *Return to Spoon River*, at the Torino Film Festival. This is by no means a comprehensive list of *Spoon River*–inspired works.

6. In "The Genesis of Spoon River," Masters says, "I regret that I used this name [Whedon], because there was an Editor Whedon there, a mild harmless man. But the piece could never be identified with his character and so he was not really hurt (42). [Seriously?]

7. A good argument could be made for considering *Spoon River Anthology* to be a modernist work because the poems relate an overarching narrative in an achronological, nonlinear way that interweaves several related stories. Briefly, Ralph Rhodes, Thomas Rhodes's son, caused his father's bank to fail by borrowing money to purchase commodities on margin. Thomas Rhodes and his son then framed their cashier, George Reece, who was convicted and imprisoned. Through his control of the courts and several business connections in town, Thomas Rhodes blocked compensatory payments to workers injured on the job, skimmed off the interest earned by public monies, and avoided paying taxes. When Butch Weldy was gravely injured in an accident at the canning factory, Rhodes used his influence with Justice Arnett to make sure that Weldy could not recover damages. Coolbaugh Whedon took bribes to keep such information out of the news. The Reverend Abner Peet and Deacon Taylor, as

well as Mayor A. D. Blood, composed key elements of the power structure in Spoon River that supported Thomas Rhodes and his cronies.

8. Banker Walter Hancock Rhodes, who was an officer of the Lewiston National Bank from 1894 until 1907, could also have been a source for Thomas Rhodes, as Rhodes's bank rivaled the one in which Hardin Masters held stock (Hallwas, Notes 394).

9. Hallwas points out that although Masters does not appear to condemn Rhodes, he actually does, as he was a follower of the philosopher Benedict de Spinoza, and the Spoon River poems constitute his Spinozistic quest for salvation. Hallwas writes, "[T]he poem is deeply ironic from a Spinozistic perspective. The questing liberals and intellectuals are tumbling into the air and splitting into atoms because they are becoming free from bondage to the self and unified with God-as-Nature, while Rhodes is still imprisoned in his self-bound perspective" (Introduction 27, 24).

10. See "Minerva Jones," "Zenas Witt," "Margaret Fuller Slack," "John Horace Burleson," "Rev. Abner Peet," "Ida Chicken," "Amos Sibley," "Carl Hamblin," "Seth Compton," and "Ippolit Konovaloff." Also see the poems that affirm books and reading as spiritually and intellectually nourishing, inspirational, and empowering: "Judson Stoddard," "Gustav Richter," "Lydia Humphrey," "Alfonso Churchill," "The Village Atheist," "Scholfield Huxley," "William Jones," "Immanuel Ehrenhardt," "Tennessee Claflin Shope," "Alfred Moir," "Thomas Trevelyan," "Jonathan Swift Somers," and "State's Attorney Fallas." A future essay could fruitfully explore this dialectic.

Works Cited

A. C. H. [Alice Corbin Henderson]. Review of *Spoon River Anthology*, by Edgar Lee Masters. *Poetry: A Magazine of Verse*, vol. 6, no. 3, June 1915, pp. 145–49.

Alter, Alexandra. "Author as Conscript in the Book-Ban War." *The New York Times*, 4 Sept. 2023, p. C5.

———, and Elizabeth A. Harris. "Booksellers, Publishers and Authors Fighting Texas' Limits on Books." *The New York Times*, 25 July 2023, p. A16.

———, Gilbert Cruz, and Elizabeth A. Harris. "A Fraught Chapter in American Education." *The New York Times*, 9 May 2023, p. A2.

Balint, Benjamin. "A Nation's Narrator." Review of *Amos Oz*, by Robert Alter. *Wall Street Journal*, 23–24 Sept. 2023, p. C11.

Braithwaite, William Stanley. "The Soul of Spoon River." Review of *Spoon River Anthology*, by Edgar Lee Masters. *Boston Evening Transcript*, 1 May 1915, part 3, p. 8.

Burgess, Charles E. *The Use of Local Lore in* Spoon River Anthology. 1969. Southern Illinois U, MA thesis.

———. "Masters and Some Mentors." *Papers on Language and Literature*, vol. 10, no. 2, spring 1974, pp. 175–201.

———. "Spoon River: Politics and Poetry." *Papers on Language and Literature*, vol. 23, no. 3, summer 1987, pp. 347–63.

Chandran, K. Narayanda. "Revolt from the Grave: *Spoon River Anthology* by Edgar Lee Masters." *Midwest Quarterly*, vol. 29, no. 4, summer 1988, pp. 438–47.

Chiaet, Julianne. "Novel Finding: Reading Literary Fiction Improves Empathy." *Scientific American*, 4 Oct. 2013, www.scientificamerican.com/article/novel-finding-reading-literary-fiction-improves-empathy/. Accessed 8 Nov. 2018.

Childs, Herbert Ellsworth. "Agrarianism and Sex: Edgar Lee Masters and the Modern Spirit." *Sewanee Review*, vol. 41, no. 3, July–Sept. 1933, pp. 331–43.

Dell, Floyd. "Spoon River People." *The New Republic*, vol. II, no. 24, part 2, 17 Apr. 1915, pp. 14–15. Spring Literary Review.

Earnest, Ernest. "Spoon River Revisited." *Western Humanities Review*, vol. 21, no. 1, winter 1967, pp. 59–65.

Exman, Bridgette. "This Summer, I Became the Book-Banning Monster of Iowa." *The New York Times*, 3 Sept. 2023, p. SR4. Editorial.

Flanagan, John T. *The Spoon River Poet and His Critics*. Scarecrow P, 1974.

Gilman, Lawrence. "Moving-Picture Poetry." Review of *Spoon River Anthology*, by Edgar Lee Masters. *The North American Review*, vol. 202, no. 717, Aug. 1915, pp. 271–76.

Glaspell, Susan. Unpublished typescript 1-2. Susan Glaspell Papers, Henry and Albert Berg Collection, New York Public Library.

Hallwas, John E. Introduction. Masters, *Spoon River*, pp. 1–79.

———. Notes to the Poems. Masters, *Spoon River*, pp. 363–436.

Harris, Elizabeth A., and Alexandra Alter. "Efforts to Ban Books Are Rapidly Increasing at Public Libraries." *The New York Times*, 22 Sept. 2023, p. A22.

Hartley, Lois. *Spoon River Revisited*. Ball State Teachers College, 1963. Ball State Monographs.

———. "Edgar Lee Masters, Political Essayist." *Journal of the Illinois State Historical Society*, vol. 57, no. 3, autumn 1964, pp. 249–60.

Hiaasen, Carl. "Swamp Things." *Vanity Fair*, no. 752, Oct. 2023, pp. 40–41.

Howells, William Dean. "Editor's Easy Chair." *Harper's Magazine*, vol. 131, no. 1284, Sept. 1915, pp. 634–35.

"A Human Anthology of Spoon River." Review of *Spoon River Anthology*, by Edgar Lee Masters. *The New York Times Book Review*, 18 July 1915, p. 261.

Hurt, James. "The Sources of the Spoon: Edgar Lee Masters and the *Spoon River Anthology*." *The Centennial Review*, vol. 24, no. 4, fall 1980, pp. 403–31.

"Illinois Becomes First State in U.S. to Outlaw Book Bans in Libraries: 'Regimes Ban Books, Not Democracies.'" *CBS News*, 13 June 2023, www.cbsnews.com/news/illinois-outlaws-book-bans-libraries/. Accessed 12 July 2023.

Kakutani, Michiko. "'Lincoln in the Bardo' Shows a President Haunted by Grief." Review of *Lincoln in the Bardo*, by George Saunders. *The New York Times*, 6 Feb. 2017, pp. C1, C3.

Masters, Edgar Lee. *Across Spoon River*. 1936. U of Illinois P, 1991.

———. "The Genesis of Spoon River." *The American Mercury*, vol. 28, no. 109, Jan. 1933, pp. 38–55.

———. *The New Star Chamber and Other Essays*, annotated edition. Edited by Jason Stacy et al., Southern Illinois UP, pp. 23–35.

———. *Spoon River Anthology: An Annotated Edition*. Edited by John E. Hallwas, U of Illinois P, 1992.

Mulvey, Irene. "Defending Academic Libraries." *Academe*, vol. 109, no. 2, spring 2023, p. 56.

Nafisi, Azar. *Reading Lolita in Tehran: A Memoir in Books*. Random House, 2003.

Narveson, Robert. "*Spoon River Anthology*: An Introduction." *MidAmerica*, vol. 7, 1980, pp. 52–72.

N. H. D [Nathan Haskell Doyle]. "Spoon River and Greece, Source of Mr. Masters' 'Anthology' in Ancient Times." Review of *Spoon River Anthology*, by Edgar Lee Masters. *Boston Evening Transcript*, 30 June 1915, p. 22.

"Poetry, American and Foreign." Review of *Spoon River Anthology*, by Edgar Lee Masters. *American Review of Reviews*, vol. 51, no. 6, June 1915, pp. 758–59.

Primeau, Ronald. Preface. *Beyond Spoon River: The Legacy of Edgar Lee Masters*. U of Texas P, 1981, pp. ix–xii.

———. Afterword. *Spoon River Anthology*. 1915. Signet Classics, 2007, pp. 295–305.

Quinn, Joanna. *The Whalebone Theatre*. Alfred A. Knopf, 2022.

Russell, Herbert K. *Edgar Lee Masters: A Biography*. U of Illinois P, 2001.

Scanlan, Laura Wolff. "How the Once-Banned *Spoon River Anthology* Made a Comeback in Lewiston." *Humanities*, vol. 36, no. 6, Nov./Dec. 2015, pp. 6–7.

Schuessler, Jennifer. "Powerful Weapons in Their Pockets." *The New York Times*, 7 Oct. 2023, pp. C1, C6.

Snouffer, Mary S., and Patricia Rinehart. "Poetry for the Reluctant." *English Journal*, vol. 50, no. 1, Jan. 1961, pp. 44–46.

Stacy, Jason. *Spoon River America: Edgar Lee Masters and the Myth of the American Small Town*. U of Illinois P, 2021.

———. Introduction. Masters, *The New Star Chamber*, pp. 1–18.

Van Doren, Carl. "The Revolt from the Village: 1920." *The Nation*, vol. 113, 21 Oct. 1921, pp. 407–12.

Wilder, Thornton. *Our Town*. 1938. HarperCollins, 2003.

SINCLAIR LEWIS'S *MAIN STREET* AND AMERICA'S CULTURAL DIVIDE

Ralph Goldstein

"It is hard to escape the conclusion," complained book critic W. J. McNally in the *Minneapolis Sunday Tribune*, "that Mr. Lewis is simply insensible to the beauties and poetries bequeathed us by the gods." Four months after *Main Street*'s October 1920 publication, McNally joined a chorus of others who took umbrage over the novel's depictions of the rural Midwest. Prominent eastern critics were not among them. Brooklyn-born columnist Heywood Broun praised it as a convincing "picture of the life of an entire community [where Lewis] hears even better than he sees," and from Baltimore, H. L. Mencken lauded Lewis for "attacking Philistinism with Philistine weapons" (139). Sales of the book skyrocketed. Carl Van Doren noted that thousands "read it merely to quarrel with it; other thousands to find out what all the world was talking about; still other thousands to rejoice in a satire which they thought to be at the expense of stupid people never once identified with themselves" (410). McNally went on to acknowledge *Main Street*'s strengths, its critique of bourgeois values and the candid portrayal of an individual in conflict with her community, and he felt Minnesotans could be proud of their native son's literary achievement. Less charitable were the editorial writers and church pastors who railed against Lewis, and the educators and librarians who feared the book's impact on youth. Beyond reflecting the erosion of rural prominence and rise of urban influence, *Main Street* senses the shifts and schisms in early twentieth-century politics, religion, and social and sexual mores, rifts Lewis continued to explore in later novels. Now, resistance to gender equity, hostility to science, pressure on librarians to withdraw certain books, and politicians trafficking in anger and resentment as they exploit fear of "the other" seem all too familiar.

At the center of *Main Street* is Carol Milford, born not on the prairie but in Mankato, Minnesota, in whose "garden-sheltered streets and aisles of elms is white and green New England reborn" (S. Lewis 6). Moving to Minneapolis with her father and sister when her mother died, orphaned two years later by her father's passing, she develops a liberal, independent streak at church-affiliated Blodgett College, where she strives "to be different from brisk efficient book-ignoring people" (7). After graduation, "not unhappy and … not exhilarated" (10) as a St. Paul librarian, she meets at a friend's Sunday supper Doctor Will Kennicott visiting from rural Gopher Prairie, who after a brief engagement urges her as his wife to make great changes in the town.

The view from the train taking Carol to her new home unsettles her. Two stops from Gopher Prairie she notices ramshackle buildings with "clapboards painted red and bilious yellow" (23) and a cattle pen beside the station. Will concedes that such "Dutch burgs *are* kind of slow," but admires its most prosperous citizen who lives in "a dandy great big yellow brick house" (24, italics in original) while holding mortgages on farms and half the town. Carol wonders why such wealth isn't put back into the area, seeding her suspicion about exploitative relations among farmers, merchants, bankers, and real estate speculators, which intensifies as she continues to live in Gopher Prairie, attracting to her, and by extension to Lewis, accusations of socialist sympathies.

Upon arrival, Gopher Prairie to Carol is "merely an enlargement of all the hamlets which they had been passing" (26). Disturbed by the "dinginess and lugubriousness and airlessness" of Will's house, Carol resolves that she'll "make it all jolly" (30) and steps out to get her "first view of the empire I'm going to conquer!" (32). Taking only thirty-two minutes to cover the town, "she stood at the corner of Main Street and Washington Avenue and despaired:

> Main Street with its two-story brick shops, its story-and-a-half wooden residences, its muddy expanse from walk to walk, its huddle of Fords and lumber-wagons, was too small to absorb her. The broad, straight, unenticing gashes of the streets let in the grasping prairie on every side. She realized the vastness and the emptiness of the land. The skeleton iron windmill on the farm a few blocks away, at the north end of Main Street,

was like ribs of a dead cow. She thought of the coming of the Northern winter, when the unprotected houses would crouch together in terror of storms galloping out of that wild waste. They were so small and weak, the little brown houses. They were shelters for sparrows, not homes for warm laughing people. (33)

But Carol is not insensible to the resplendent countryside beyond the town, as this passage recounting her first duck hunting trip attests:

They drove home under the sunset. Mounds of straw, and wheat-stacks like bee-hives, stood out in startling rose and gold, and the green-tufted stubble glistened. As the vast girdle of crimson darkened, the fulfilled land became autumnal in deep reds and browns. The black road before the buggy turned to a faint lavender, then was blotted to uncertain grayness. Cattle came in a long line up to the barred gates of the farmyards, and over the resting land was a dark glow.

Carol had found the dignity and greatness which had failed her in Main Street. (58)

Gradually happy in her home, proud to be acknowledged by townspeople as "Mrs. Doc Kennicott," appreciative of "the homely ease of village life" (63), Carol receives a disturbing visit from schoolteacher Vida Sherwin who lets her know what she's up against in her reform quest: the gossips say she's flippant to merchants, eccentric in her home decoration, too friendly with her Swedish maid, a frivolous dresser, a show-off who refers to places farther than Minneapolis, says "American" instead of "Ammurrican" (95), and doesn't go to church often enough. Hurt by the criticism, Carol still moves ahead with beautification plans, which elderly Mrs. Champ Perry dampens. Originally coming by ox-cart from Sauk Centre to Gopher Prairie with Mr. Champ when there were only a few log cabins and a stockade, living for a time in a house roofed with hay, Mrs. Champ thinks refurbishing the city hall, library, and public women's restroom is unnecessary. As for Carol's idea for town-sponsored dances, Mrs. Champ opines that dances at fraternal orders suffice "even if some of the lodges don't always welcome a lot of these foreigners and hired help" (136). Further, Mrs. Champ shares with Carol a sampling of her other fundamental beliefs, that "all this new-fangled science [is] ruining our young men in colleges ... [t]he Republican Party is the agent of the Lord and of the Baptist Church in temporal affairs ... socialists ought to be hanged ... [t]here would be no more trouble or discontent in the world if everybody worked as hard as Pa did when he cleared our first farm" (153).

Carol organizes a community theater troupe that disbands after its sole performance of "The Girl from Kankakee." A troupe member, lawyer Guy Pollock, formerly of New York City, offers himself as a victim of the "village virus" that "infects ambitious people who stay too long in the provinces ... lawyers and doctors and ministers and college-bred merchants ... who have had a glimpse of the world that thinks and laughs, but have returned to their swamp" (156). Carol gives birth to a son, Hugh, and is cheered by motherhood but over time sours on her neighbors, viewing them as a "savorless people, gulping tasteless food ... listening to mechanical music, saying mechanical things ... and viewing themselves as the greatest race in the world" (265). She's made more uneasy by Reverend Zitterel's sermon in the Baptist church, where he rails against the unions and Farmers' Nonpartisan League, calls "economics and socialism and science ... a disguise for atheism," and laments that "this vain generation of young girls (thinks) more about wearing silk stockings than about minding their mothers and learning to bake a good loaf of bread" (330).

The rise in the price of wheat near the end of World War I leads to a squabble that ruptures the Kennicotts' marriage, already fractured by Carol's romantic dalliance with a young tailor and Will's adultery with a friend's wife. Much more than the farmers, the townsmen—"millers, real-estate men, lawyers, merchants, and Dr. Will Kennicott"—enriched themselves by buying land and selling the next day at a profit, and within three months Will had made "more than four times as much as society paid him for healing the sick" (413). When Will and Carol learn that a neighboring town's sheriff led a mob to prevent a political organizer from speaking to local farmers, many of them German and Scandinavian immigrants, Carol questions the action's legality; but Will, using an ethnic slur and accusing the farmers of sedition in wartime, declares when it's a matter "of defending Americanism and our constitutional rights, it's justifiable to set aside ordinary procedure" (419). After he reproaches Carol for her views, her years-long resentment of being "a woman with a working brain and no work" (85) save housekeeping and motherhood makes her finally erupt and decide to leave.

With son Hugh she spends two years in Washington, D.C., finding work in a government office and volunteering to address envelopes for a militant suffrage organization. Will visits, they have a loving reunion, and he returns home. Later, at dinner with a "generalissima of suffrage," who has devoted her life entirely to the cause, Carol doubts she's capable of such sacrifice and wonders aloud if she should return to Gopher Prairie, to which the leader suggests:

"Your Middlewest is double-Puritan—prairie Puritan on top of New England Puritan ... There's one attack you can make on it, perhaps the only kind that accomplishes much anywhere: you can keep on looking at one thing after another in your home and church and bank, and ask why it is, and who first laid down the law that it had to be that way. If enough of us do this impolitely enough, then we'll become civilized in merely twenty thousand years or so, instead of having to wait the two hundred thousand years that my cynical anthropologist friends allow." (441)

Pregnant with her second child, a girl, Carol returns home to a reconciled marriage. After her baby is born Carol is uncertain whether her daughter is "to become a feminist leader or marry a scientist or both" (448) but confident about what the girl "will see and meddle with before she dies in the year 2000!" When Will asks if she's finally "tired of fretting and stewing and experimenting," Carol replies, "I haven't even started" (450).

Clergymen assailed *Main Street* and its author. At Hobart College, the Right Reverend Charles H. Brent, Bishop of the Episcopal Diocese of Western New

York, attacked it as a "pagan book" causing "foreboding among the older men of the country." In contrast with what he called the "idealistic character of great literature," best exemplified by the Bible, modern literature, including Lewis's novel, offers "little more than sodden depression" ("Brent Raps"). Reverend Lee J. Beynon of Calvary Baptist Church in Clifton, New Jersey, found the residents of Gopher Prairie "vulgar, jealous, small-minded, narrow visioned, penurious, gossipy, and intellectually incapable of enjoying the finer pleasures of life." To him, Lewis had dragged Christianity "in the mire," that a sermon like Rev. Zitterell's has never been made in a Baptist church "since the time of Jesus," and American prestige would be damaged if the novel is translated into other languages ("Pastor Beynon").[1] A more elegant, measured but similarly forceful critique came from Rev. Albert W. Palmer, whose sermon at Honolulu's Central Union Church was reprinted in the Arts section of the *Honolulu Star Bulletin*. While initially lauding the book's photographic realism, particularly the portrayal of the town's "herd-like conservatism and its cruel and stupid intolerance, coupled with its sublime self-satisfaction and conceit," he regrets that as a satire it leaves out "the good and the lovely" qualities of Gopher Prairies across the country known for their supportive churches, effective schools, and neighborliness among townspeople. He's unduly harsh on Carol, seeing her as weak and "hopelessly adrift," falling into self-pity after her first try at reform. The clue as to why Lewis characterized the town as he did, Rev. Palmer insists, is in the author's "embittered soul" and his social philosophy that is "Marxian socialist with Bolshevik tendencies ... out to smash smug, conceited, vulgar, prosperous, capitalistic America." As "a moral anarchist," Lewis's hatred of Puritanism is palpable, and his book is infected with "a widely prevalent disease in modern fiction—the Freudian hypothesis" that locates sexual repression as the source of all unhappiness. Finally, in the face of *Main Street*'s popularity, Rev. Palmer calls for moral and spiritual uplift of marriages "characterized by fidelity and a love which though less volcanic and turbulent grows deeper" ("What's the Matter").

Reflecting the ambivalence shown earlier by its critic W. J. McNally, The *Minneapolis Star Tribune* noted without comment that the wait list to check out the book from the Minneapolis library had reached 171 ("'Main Street' Breaks") but on the same day editorialized about "the present cult of the disagreeable … a literary fad … the modern tendency to describe things which are not at all bad as really terrible" ("Fiction with a Grouch"). Days later the *Star Tribune* relayed the religious weekly *The Continent*'s condemnation of Lewis's method of "select(ing) every item that is sordid, mean, unlovely, insolent, malicious, sensual, degrading, morally anarchistic, irreverent and faithless … [to] work up a tale bringing every one of these elements by turn into unpleasant prominence" ("Scandalizing").[2] In June the *Sunday Star Tribune* touted the Sauk Centre Country Club's donation of land for a tourist park open to the public and the efforts of 150 volunteers who cleared and graded the land, sank a well and put in a pump, as "giv(ing) the lie to Carol" ("Gopher Prairie's Answer"). Then in August at the bottom of the *Sunday Tribune*'s front page ("Grand Jury Probe"), underneath headlines of a graft investigation, Ireland heading for civil war, a teenage girl fending off seven Mexican bandits, fear of a railroad labor strike, and immigrants defrauded of shipping charges, is news that the library board of Alexandria, Minnesota, some twenty-six miles northwest of Sauk Centre, withdrew its copy of *Main Street* from the shelves ("Library Censors Bar").[3] Animus against *Main Street* continued. The *Indianapolis Star* reminded readers that American towns must first satisfy basic necessities, after which they add beauty and luxury "so that even little brides who have lived in cities and therefore feel themselves cultured can abide them" ("A Central 'Main Street'"). The library of Kinston, North Carolina, banned *Main Street* because "everything that happened in 'Main Street' might have happened in Kinston" ("Kinston Sees Itself"). And at a November conference, keynoter Dr. Richard Burton urged Minnesota educators to "rise up in their wrath and refuse to be fooled by a semblance of good writing into approving a book that is mean and disagreeable and untrue" ("'Main Street' Is Criticised").

Barnstorming the country to promote the book, Lewis showed he could give criticism as well as take it. At New York's Town Hall, he scolded the public for not reading beyond headlines, deplored censorship, and credited the city as a place where "a stranger can stand up and abuse New York and get away with it" ("New York Doesn't Read"). Lecturing to students at the University of Illinois, Lewis proclaimed, "I love Main Street.... No man can write a whole book on a subject he does not love. It is because I do love the small country town that I want to see that which is not perfect corrected" ("Lewis Introduces"). Lewis's host on the Urbana campus, Professor Stuart P. Sherman, was later part of a three-judge panel recommending *Main Street* to win the Pulitzer Prize, a decision Pulitzer trustees overturned and chose instead Edith Wharton's *Age of Innocence* as the novel best representing "the wholesome atmosphere of American life, and the highest standard of American manners and manhood" (S. Lewis "Letter" 19). Lewis, who revered Wharton and would dedicate *Babbitt* to her, wrote to congratulate her. In reply, she shared with Lewis her disgust that the trustees voted against *Main Street* because it "offended a number of prominent persons in the Middle West," that "the kind Appletons have smothered me," and she despaired that she was "being rewarded ... for uplifting American morals" (qtd. in Schorer 312). Lewis's admiration for Wharton was requited. "He really *is* an artist," she told R. W. B. Lewis. "[T]he average modern novelist could live for a year on Sinclair Lewis's leavings" (qtd. in Lingeman 184).

Five years later, Lewis declined the honor when the Pulitzer jury and trustees voted to give the Prize to *Arrowsmith*, Lewis's novel of a courageous, epidemic-fighting young doctor. In a widely publicized statement, Lewis urged other writers to be wary of accepting literary taste-makers' gifts, as doing so could lead them to "become safe, polite, obedient, and sterile" ("Letter" 20). But that didn't stop him from going to Stockholm in 1930, the first American to win the Nobel Prize for Literature. In his Nobel acceptance, titled "The American Fear of Literature," he argued that his compatriots reject literature that isn't a glorification of everything American, and he mocked his parochial critics, wondering if they would call for the US marines to land in Stockholm to protect their literary interests (5).

Lewis famously said that while he loved America, he often didn't like it. With regard to women's suffrage, he literally walked the walk. As part of a small group of male allies who paraded up Fifth Avenue with thousands of women in support of the 1915 New York women's suffrage initiative, he attracted jeers and garbage thrown from onlookers. In her memoir, Lewis's first wife, Gracie, a passionate suffrage advocate, remembered him shouting, "[I]f a human being who was a man had a right to vote, a human being who was a woman had the same right," and she explained his advocacy as based on hatred of any kind of prohibition (G. Lewis 68). In an unpublished autobiographical sketch found among his papers after his death, Lewis develops the irritation he'd later point at satiric targets. About himself he states,

> He hates, equally, politicians who lie and bully and steal under cover of windy and banal eloquence; … manufacturers who pose as philanthropists while underpaying their workmen; professors who in wartime try to prove that the enemy are all fiends, and novelists who are afraid to say what seems to them the truth. ("Self-Portrait" 48)

After Lewis's mockery of social conformity in *Babbitt* and religious fundamentalism in *Elmer Gantry*, he focused on systemic change in his 1933 novel *Ann Vickers*, the title character of which champions prison reform and government-funded social work. Ann's abortion and adultery caused Ireland to ban the book ("Books Banned"), Spain to bowdlerize it in translation (Goldstein),[4] and enforcers of the Hays production code to demand the elimination of those plot elements from the 1934 film version ("John Cromwell"). Part of the inspiration for this book came from Lewis and wife Gracie's friendship with Katherine Houghton Hepburn who, with Margaret Sanger, founded the American Birth Control League, which evolved into Planned Parenthood.

He hurried to complete in advance of the 1936 election *It Can't Happen Here*, his tale of fascism come to America, where radio preachers inflame the "forgotten" people, books are burned, racist and anti-Semitic laws passed, and war sabers rattled against Mexico. Because he'd written it so quickly, Lewis acknowledged his stylistic failings at a tribute dinner given by the left-leaning League of American Writers after the book's publication: "Boys," he said, "I love you all, and a writer loves to have his latest book praised. But let me tell you, it isn't a very good book—I've done better books—and furthermore, I don't believe any of you have read the book; if you had, you would have seen I was telling all of you to go to hell" (qtd. in Schorer

611). Lewis never joined the League; selective about his commitments, he used politics but was not used by it (Aaron 404). A proposed film version of the novel suffered so many demands for changes from the Production Code Association that the studio cancelled the project (Black 185).

After 1936 came and went without Lewis's nightmare materializing, he didn't stop mocking what he saw as insidious forms of mass manipulation. Unlike the despot of *It Can't Happen Here*, the title character of his 1943 novel *Gideon Planish* is a college professor turned behind-the-scenes exploiter of voter and consumer vulnerabilities. Leaving academe for a philanthropic organization, Gideon exudes over his dreams "of crystallizing public opinion … and molding public opinion … and [forming] pressure groups to exert influence …" (158–60). These inspirational lines include verbiage identical to the writing of the real public relations magnate Edward Bernays offering instruction on "manipulating the social machinery which controls the opinions and habits of the masses" (37).[5] Promoting bogus philanthropy, Gideon supervises the distribution of anti-union and right-wing xenophobic pamphlets, with titles such as "The Cross and the Stars and Stripes—or the Assassin's Dagger and the Crossed Hammer and Sickle—WHICH?" (270), parodying ultranationalist race-baiter Gerald L. K. Smith's fund-raising magazine *The Cross and the Flag*, which began publishing in 1942 (Jeansonne 429).[6] Gideon and his wife Peony live beyond their means,[7] so to rise above their mountainous debt Peony suggests to Gideon that he "consolidate a string of small colleges … like chainstores (with) advertising and profits" (206). After all, they first met at Kinnikinick, a private college which Lewis ridicules as a business "[with] sales and advertising departments" (54). And where, displaying the polite bigotry of the times, Gideon insists to a student "that we of the superior race are … destined to rule, tenderly but firmly, all the yellow, brown and black hordes" (121).

The April 8, 1944, issue of the *Saturday Review of Literature* featured Bernard DeVoto's indictment of 1920s writers including Lewis: "Never in any country or any age had writers so misrepresented their culture, never had they been so unanimously wrong. Never had writers been so completely separated from the experiences that alone give life and validity to literature" (qtd. in Lewis "Fools, Liars"

153–54). In the following week's issue Lewis belittled DeVoto's charge, offering as similarly unprovable that "the major writers of the twenties, men who so loved their country that they were willing to report its transient dangers and stupidities, have been as valuable an influence as America has ever known" ("Fools, Liars" 162).

Not chastened by DeVoto or other critics, Lewis doubled down on creating fictive representations of what he saw to be American dangers and stupidities. In advance of the national reckoning with civil rights, Lewis derides racism in his 1947 novel *Kingsblood Royal*, where World War II veteran Neil Kingsblood discovers a letter in which an ancestor describes himself as "a full-blooded Negro born in Martinique" (68). Neil, who had spoken racist epithets, internalized beliefs in white supremacy, tries but fails to keep knowledge of his lineage away from the citizenry of Grand Republic, Minnesota. Once the news spreads among whites, he is pressured to resign from his job and his family is urged to sell their home. Violence ensues when they refuse, and they are taken to jail.

As background, Lewis knew of the murder trials twenty years earlier of Dr. Ossian Sweet, who used self-defense against a white mob trying to oust his family from their home. Through his friendship with NAACP president Walter White, who organized the defense of Dr. Sweet led by Clarence Darrow, Lewis met prominent Black writers (Cooney) and he served on the Federal Writers Project panel that helped launch the career of Richard Wright (Buckhout), who later claimed Lewis as a major influence (Schorer 812) and whose 1945 memoir *Black Boy* Lewis praised in a review titled "Gentlemen, This Is Revolution" (76).[8]

Kingsblood Royal struck a nerve, especially in the South, where Random House was warned not to market it in the smaller cities, and Atlanta and New Orleans booksellers concealed copies unless customers specifically asked for them (Sova 234). In 2002, nearly six decades after a predecessor panned the book, Brent Staples in *The New York Times* declared that Lewis's literary reputation had risen again. Linking *Kingsblood Royal* to Lewis's other societal critiques, Jennifer Delton in 2003 noted "the passion that fueled the novel came … from a profound sense of cultural disillusion, in which racism was but a symptom of a larger failing" (327). More recently, in an otherwise generous appraisal of Lewis's life and legacy, the late editor Robert Gottlieb failed to consider midcentury riots over integrated housing and persistent de facto segregation before condemning *Kingsblood Royal*'s central premise as "preposterous."

After attacking racial hierarchies in *Kingsblood Royal*, Lewis in his penultimate novel, *The God-Seeker*, ridicules cultural hegemony in the nineteenth-century encounter between indigenous people and white evangelists. While researching for the novel at the Minnesota Historical Society Lewis made his final visit to Sauk Centre, where at a Chamber of Commerce dinner he praised the pioneers but criticized their wasteful land management and what he called their "philosophy of prejudice" (Lingeman 526). Aaron Gadd, the God-seeker for whom the novel is titled, joins the Minnesota settlement of Balthazar Harge, whose mission is to aid natives, described by him as "hell-flamed, gorge-raising, murderous, adulterous, Sabbath-breaking sons of Belial, ... climb to civilization [and] see on their dark and rugged prairies the light of the kindled cross" (45–46).[9] Lewis gives voice to historical personages Thomas Smith Williamson, who says of the natives, "Satan has, literally and scientifically ... made these people his own" (118), and Stephen Return Riggs, who allows that some "Sioux Christians ... are just as good as white men, in their *place*" (119, italics in original). Aaron eventually questions his previously received notions of natives as soulless savages, befriends Oberlin-educated Black Wolf, and marries Selene, the biracial daughter of a white trader and a Dakota Sioux woman who fled to escape her husband's brutality. They raise their children in the rapidly expanding St. Paul of the 1850s, where Aaron has co-founded a construction firm, encourages his employees to unionize, finds shelter for a runaway slave, and later hires him as an equal among the other workers. Often criticized for failing to offer solutions, Lewis here embraces secular inclusion to resolve the ills he identifies.[10]

Lewis's name lately surfaces in odd places. In Jane Mayer's 2016 study *Dark Money*, she describes the activism of fossil fuel billionaires Charles and David Koch as "cloaked in secrecy and presented as philanthropy" (3–4). Mayer learned that the brothers' libertarian notions were fostered at a so-called Freedom School, where the eldest brother, Freddie, who until his death in 2020 was uninvolved in his siblings' political activity, thought the school's curriculum was "bilge" and the school's founder "reminded him of the con artists in Sinclair Lewis's novels" (45).

Hamlin Garland, who served on the 1921 Pulitzer jury recommending *Main Street* for the Prize, voted unenthusiastically for it, wondering if the book was merely "a piece of clever journalism which will be dead in six months" (qtd. in Oehlschlaeger 411). The novel's reach has extended much longer, but by some measures attention to it has waned. A sampling of appearances on college syllabi of works by midwestern writers shows *The Great Gatsby*'s 4,019, *A Raisin in the Sun*'s 2,599, *Winesburg, Ohio*'s 656, and *Spoon River Anthology*'s 170, dwarfing *Main Street*'s meagre 11 ("Titles"). And, ignoring Lewis, a Heartland school district recently flagged for potential banning 397 books, including by his fellow Nobelists Pearl Buck, William Faulkner, Ernest Hemingway, and Toni Morrison (Higgins). But according to Sauk Centre High School English teacher Dana Boschee, *Main Street* has been taught periodically for over three recent decades in Lewis's hometown. He recalled that students saw Lewis as "quite the smart-aleck with many targets to make fun of [such as] sexist and anti-immigrant beliefs, which were easy to connect to current events. And of course we looked into hypocrisies which is something young people are keen to identify, especially in the older generations."

Midway through her experience in Washington, Carol Kennicott realizes she has gained greater courage and poise to face external obstacles. We might consider this meditation of hers, bringing some calm and maybe even some levity as we go through the challenging days ahead:

And why, she began to ask, did she rage at individuals? Not individuals but institutions are the enemies, and they most afflict the disciples who the most generously serve them. They insinuate their tyranny under a hundred guises and pompous names, such as Polite Society, the Family, the Church, Sound Business, the Party, the Country, the Superior White Race; and the only defense against them, Carol beheld, is unembittered laughter. (430)

The Sinclair Lewis Society

Notes

1. "By 1930, eleven of Lewis's thirteen books had been translated into Russian, German, and Polish; seven into Hungarian, Danish, Norwegian, and Czech; six into French; four into Dutch; two into Spanish; and one, *Babbitt*, into Italian and Hebrew. Most of Lewis's books had also been translated into Swedish." See Hutchisson (204).

2. *The Continent's* article may have influenced Reverend Palmer, mentioned above, as some of its terms echo in the sermon he penned five months later.

3. *The Sauk Centre Herald* reported on September 15, 1921 that the Alexandria library returned to the publisher its defective copy but did not ban the book ("Alexandria Denies Banning").

4. Depicting Lewis's novel as "rooted in the vibrant changes in North America and Europe interweaving women's suffrage, feminism, pacifism, and social equality," Spanish sociologist Marin Gómez finds in this novel a "literature of extraordinary richness of social work history, up to that time unexplored" (6).

5. Lewis incorporated into Gideon Planish's meditation on public service the titles of two of Bernays's tracts: *Crystallizing Public Opinion* and "Molding Public Opinion" (158).

6. At the time Lewis was writing *Gideon Planish*, Smith's speeches in the Twin Cities attracted large crowds (Freedman 203).

7. Peony's purchases with or without Gideon's agreement include a Chippendale cabinet, Chinese rug, rock-crystal lamp, five hundred shares in a diamond mine, leather floor-cushion, French imitation porcelain mantel clock, new Buick, piano, radio, steel-point antique ring, portable bar, Chinese lamp, Gaugin print, cedar blanket-chest, expensive lingerie she considers an investment, and a near-diamond semi-sapphire bracelet.

8. There he calls special attention to the thesis, "bland as dynamite soup," of African American writer George Schuyler, "that there is no Negro Problem at all, but there decidedly is a Caucasian Problem" ("Gentleman, This Is Revolution" 77). Schuyler's 1931 satire ridiculing racial classifications, *Black No More*, can be seen as a precursor to Lewis's novel.

9.   To show that Harge's harsh rhetoric is similar to what can be found in historical research, Albert Tricomi in "America's Missionary Evangelicalism in Sinclair Lewis's *The God-Seeker*" cites Ayako Uchida: "Ayako Uchida's examination of the Protestant missions among the Dakota Sioux, a study that exhibits no knowledge whatsoever of *The God-Seeker*, draws extensively from Dakota missionary diaries during the period that Lewis represents. These repeatedly depict the Indians as 'backsliding,' polygamous, devil-worshipping lovers of the 'savage life, full of 'animal excitement' in their killing, scalp dancing, and wild song" (71). For Tricomi, the novel's source of enduring relevance is its depiction of an "ideology that continues to exert its influence over the national psyche" and lends support to modern-day crusades against so-called "alien regimes" (68).

10. Referred to in *The God-Seeker*, Minneapolis's Lake Calhoun (named for slavery advocate and War Secretary John C. Calhoun) reverted by administrative decree in 2017 to its Dakota name, Bde Maka Ska. Subsequent challenges to the decree ended when a 2020 decision by the Minnesota Supreme Court ruled in favor of the name change. But the fractious encounter over resources depicted in Lewis's 1949 novel goes on, most openly in resistance to the Dakota Access Pipeline (*Water Protector*).

Works Cited

Aaron, Daniel. *Writers on the Left*. Avon, 1961.

"Alexandria Denies Banning of Book." *Sauk Centre Herald*, 15 Sept. 1921, p. 1.

Bernays, Edward. *Propaganda*. Liveright, 1928.

Black, Gregory D. "Hollywood Censored: The Production Code Administration and the Hollywood Film Industry, 1930–1940." *Film History*, vol. 3, no. 3, 1989, pp. 167–89.

"Books Banned in Ireland." *The Sun* [Sydney, Australia], 15 July 1937, p. 26, trove. nla.gov.au/newspaper/article/231085536. *Trove*.

Boschee, Dana. Email to author, 19 July 2023.

"Brent Raps 'Main Street.'" *The New York Times*, 14 July 1921, p. 14.

Broun, Heywood. "Books." *The New York Tribune*, 20 Oct. 1920, p. 8.

Buckhout, Dave. "The Federal Writers Project of the WPA." *The Almanack*, 2006, www.inheritage.org/almanack/federal-writers-project-new-deal-works-progress-administration/. Accessed 16 Apr. 2018.

"A Central 'Main Street.'" *Indianapolis Star*, 20 Feb. 1921, p. 18. Editorial.

Cooney, Charles F. "Walter White and Sinclair Lewis: The History of a Literary Friendship." *Prospects*, vol. 1, 1976, pp. 63–75.

Delton, Jennifer. "Before the White Negro: Sin and Salvation in *Kingsblood Royal*." *American Literary History*, vol. 15, no. 2, summer 2003, pp. 311–33.

"Fiction with a Grouch." *Minneapolis Star Tribune*, 10 Apr. 1921, p. 50. Editorial.

Freedman, Samuel G. *Into the Bright Sunshine*. Oxford University Press, 2023.

Goldstein, Ralph. "Lewis's Lasting *Conocimiento*: *Ann Vickers* in Spain." Review of "La Historia Del Trabajo Social en La Literatura Contemporánea: *Ann Vickers* de Sinclair Lewis" by Isabel Marin Gómez, translated by Dr. Barbara Comoe Goldstein. *Sinclair Lewis Newsletter*, vol. 27, no. 2, spring 2019, p. 6.

"Gopher Prairie's Answer to Carol Kennicott." *Minneapolis Star Tribune*, 12 June 1921, p. 46. Editorial.

Gottlieb, Robert. "The Novelist Who Saw Middle America as It Really Was." *The New York Times*, 31 Dec. 2021, www.nytimes.com/2021/12/31/books/review/sinclair-lewis-babbitt-main-street.html.

"Grand Jury Probe of Graft Ring Looms." *Minneapolis Star Tribune*, 28 Aug. 1921, p. 1.

Higgins, Chris. "Iowa School District Flags 374 Books as Potentially Banned, from 'Ulysses' to 'Heartstopper.'" *The Des Moines Register*, 31 July 2023, www.desmoinesregister.com/story/news/education/2023/07/31/urbandale-school-district-iowa-book-ban-law-flagged-ulysses-color-purple-heartstopper-lgbtq-themes/70459691007/.

Hutchisson, James M. *The Rise of Sinclair Lewis, 1920–1930*. Pennsylvania State UP, 1996.

Jeansonne, Glen. "Arkansas's Minister of Hate: A Research Odyssey." *The Arkansas Historical Quarterly*, vol. 59, no. 4, winter 2000, pp. 429–35.

"John Cromwell - Biography." *IMDb*, www.imdb.com/name/nm0188669/bio/?ref_=nm_sa_1.

"Kinston Sees Itself as State's Gopher Prairie." *The News and Observer* [Raleigh], 30 Aug. 1921, p. 6.

Lewis, Grace Hegger. *With Love from Gracie: Sinclair Lewis, 1912–1925.* Harcourt, Brace and Company, 1955.

Lewis, Sinclair. "The American Fear of Literature (Nobel Prize Address)." *The Man from Main Street: Selected Essays and Other Writings, 1904–1950,* edited by Harry E. Maule and Melville Cane, Random House, 1953, pp. 3–17.

———. *Ann Vickers.* 1933. U of Nebraska P, 1994.

———. "Fools, Liars, and Mr. DeVoto." *The Man from Main Street,* pp. 153–64.

———. "Gentlemen, This Is Revolution." *Esquire,* 1 June 1945, pp. 76–77.

———. *Gideon Planish.* Random House, 1943.

———. *The God-Seeker.* Random House, 1949.

———. *It Can't Happen Here.* 1935. New American Library, 2005.

———. *Kingsblood Royal.* Random House, 1947.

———. "Letter to the Pulitzer Prize Committee." *The Man from Main Street,* pp. 18–20.

———. *Main Street.* Harcourt, Brace & Company, 1920.

———. "Self-Portrait (Berlin, August, 1927)." *The Man from Main Street,* pp. 45–51.

"Lewis Introduces Dr. Kennicott to Criticise Illinois." *The Daily Illini,* 7 Apr. 1921, pp. 1, 8.

"Library Censors Bar Lewis' 'Main Street' in Alexandria, Minn." *Minneapolis Star Tribune,* 28 Aug. 1921, p. 1.

Lingeman, Richard. *Sinclair Lewis: Rebel from Main Street.* Random House, 2002.

"'Main Street' Breaks All Records at Library by Circulation Demand." *Minneapolis Star Tribune,* 10 Apr. 1921, p. 61.

"'Main Street' Is Criticised by Dr. Burton." *Minneapolis Star Tribune,* 4 Nov. 1921, p. 16.

Marin Gómez, Isabel. "La Historia Del Trabajo Social en La Literatura Contemporánea: *Ann Vickers* de Sinclair Lewis." *Historia Social,* vol. 90, 2018, pp. 85–105.

Mayer, Jane. *Dark Money: The Hidden History of the Billionaires behind the Rise of the Radical Right.* Doubleday, 2016.

McNally, W. J. "Sinclair Lewis' 'Main Street' a Great but an Uneven Novel, Verdict of W. J. McNally." *Minneapolis Star Tribune*, 27 Feb. 1921, p. 61.

Mencken, H. L. "Consolation." *Smart Set*, Jan. 1921, pp. 138–40.

"New York Doesn't Read, Says 'Main Street' Author." *New York Herald*, 30 Mar. 1921, p. 20.

Oehlschlaeger, Fritz H. "Hamlin Garland and the Pulitzer Prize Controversy of 1921." *American Literature*, vol. 51, Nov. 1979, 409–14.

"Pastor Beynon Reviews Novel." *Passaic Daily Herald*, 9 Dec. 1921, p. 5.

"Scandalizing the Small Town." *Minneapolis Star Tribune*, 21 Apr. 1921, p. 12.

Schorer, Mark. *Sinclair Lewis: An American Life.* McGraw-Hill, 1961.

Sova, Dawn B. "*Kingsblood Royal.*" *Literature Suppressed on Social Grounds.* 3rd ed. Facts on File, 2011, pp. 233–35. *Banned Books.*

Staples, Brent. "When the Bard of 'Main Street' Turned the Kingsblood Family Black; Sinclair Lewis Exposes the Hidden 40's." *The New York Times*, 18 Aug. 2002, p. WK12. Opinion.

"Titles." *Open Syllabus Explorer*, explorer.opensyllabus.org/results-list/titles?size=50.

Tricomi, Albert H. "America's Missionary Evangelicalism in Sinclair Lewis's *The God-Seeker.*" *Studies in American Fiction*, vol. 35, no. 1, spring 2007, pp. 67–87.

Uchida, Ayako, "The Protestant Mission and Native American Response: The Case of the Dakota Mission, 1835–1862." *The Japanese Journal of American Studies*, vol. 10, 1999, pp. 153–75.

Van Doren, Carl. "The Revolt from the Village: 1920." *The Nation*, vol. 113, 12 Oct. 1921, pp. 407–12.

Water Protector Legal Collective. www.waterprotectorlegal.org/.

"What's the Matter with Main Street?" *Honolulu Star Bulletin*, 24 Sep. 1921, p. 38.

"ONE OF THE FILTHIEST BOOKS OF THE YEAR"

Hemingway's *The Sun Also Rises* as Banned Book

Donald A. Daiker

The Sun Also Rises, Ernest Hemingway's first and arguably finest novel, was banned in Boston in 1930, four years after its publication, burned in the Nazi bonfires of 1933, and banned in Ireland in 1953. In California in 1960, *The Sun Also Rises* was banned from schools in San Jose, and all of Hemingway's works were removed from Riverside school libraries. In 1960, a group called Texans for America opposed textbooks that referred students to books by Hemingway ("Bannings and Burnings"). Although PEN America reported that during the 2021–22 school year, "nearly 140 school districts in 32 states banned more than 2,500 books" (Pendharkar), *The Sun Also Rises* seems to have escaped censure. At least for now.

In the past, *The Sun Also Rises* has faced three major charges that open it to the threat of banning: (1) its language and profanity; (2) its obscenity: its focus on adultery and sexual content; and (3) its anti-Semitism. These charges are often accompanied by a claim of the novel's superficiality: *The Sun Also Rises* is "as shallow as where the water meets the sand," one anonymous critic charged.

> *"Surely you have other words in your vocabulary besides 'damn' and 'bitch.'"—Grace Hall Hemingway*

As Hemingway prepared *The Sun Also Rises* for publication, his Scribner's editor, Maxwell Perkins, afraid of censorship, cautioned him to eliminate profanity from his manuscript. According to Hemingway scholar Matthew J. Bruccoli, "Perkins's most perilous duty as Hemingway's editor was to persuade him to delete words that could not be printed by a respectable publisher …" (26). Of *The Sun Also Rises*, Perkins wrote to F. Scott Fitzgerald, "there are many words seldom if ever used before in print" (Bruccoli 40). But Hemingway resisted, telling Perkins, "I never use a word without first considering if it is replaceable" (Bruccoli 43). So when Perkins went on to recommend "large reducing so far as you rightly can the profanity, etc" (Bruccoli 43), Hemingway again stood firm, explaining, "I've tried to reduce profanity but I reduced so much profanity when writing the book that I'm afraid not much would come out" (Bruccoli 44; *Letters* 107). Then he added, tongue-in-cheek, "Perhaps we will have to consider it simply as a profane book and hope that the next book will be less profane or perhaps more sacred" (Bruccoli 44).

For Hemingway, the least reducible profanity was "bitch." It or its plural is used three times at two key points in the novel. The first two times occur just after Lady Brett Ashley has exploited Jake's love for her to persuade him to bring her to the bullfighter Pedro Romero so that the two can go off together. On their way to the assignation, Brett says, "I don't say it's right. It is right though for me. God knows I've never felt such a bitch." Moments later, Brett says, "I do feel such a bitch," which Jake acknowledges by replying, "Well" (147).[1] Two days later in Madrid, Brett tries to convince herself and Jake that it is she who has left Romero—the reverse is true (see Daiker, "Brett Couldn't Hold Him")—by declaring "I'm not going be one of these bitches that ruins children" (193). Hemingway specifically challenged Perkins's request that he eliminate the three uses of "bitch": "But in the matter of the use of Bitch by Brett—I have never used this word ornamentally nor except when it was absolutely necessary and I believe the few places where it is used *must* stand" (43, emphasis added). And so it did in the novel, because its use helps characterize Lady Ashley: first her boldness in using a forbidden term and, more important, her unbitchlike character. Brett may be self-centered and lustful, but she is not bitchy: there is nothing mean, cruel, or malicious about her. For example, she never taunts Cohn for following her about like a puppy dog or steer, and she reproves her fiancé Mike Campbell for doing so.

But if Hemingway insisted on the use of "bitch," he did yield to Perkins in one other instance. Hemingway had written that Mike, drunk, had three times called out for Jake to tell Romero "that bulls have no balls" (140, 141). Perkins, who never used profane or obscene words himself, suggested that "a particular adjunct of the Bulls, referred to a number of times by Mike, be not spelled out, but covered by a blank …" (Bruccoli 42). Hemingway agreed. "That ("no balls") can be changed—

and with no appreciable loss to—bulls have no horns" (Bruccoli 43). But in later editions of *The Sun Also Rises* "no balls" was restored.

Ernest's mother, Grace Hall Hemingway, represented everything that Perkins feared when he asked Hemingway to limit the profanity in *The Sun Also Rises*. Grace told her son that *Sun* had to be "one of the filthiest books of the year." She added that "Every page fills me with a sick loathing." She asked her son whether his vocabulary didn't extend beyond profanities like "damn" and "bitch" (*Letters* n201). In one sense Grace is right; there *is* much profanity in *Sun*, approximately 90 such instances, one roughly every two pages. On the other hand, it is profanity in its mildest form: 54 instances of "hell" and 30 instances of "damn." The novel's strongest swearword, "bastard," is used only once when Jake is at his angriest over Robert Cohn's having slept with Brett: "the lying bastard" (81). So it's difficult to understand why Grace labeled *Sun* as "filthy" since there are no sexual or scatological references to the body or bodily functions.

The profanities in *Sun* function as indices of feelings and attitudes, as clues to a character's emotional state—usually either anger or joyful anticipation. When Jake twice uses the word "hell" after being kicked under the table by Robert's girlfriend Frances, you know that he's angry even before Robert's "Don't get sore" (5, 6). When Jake uses "hell" or "damn" in four consecutive utterances, unusual for him, it's clear that Bill has angered him by asking leading questions about "this Brett business" (99). But Bill's and Jake's profanity in the following exchange are signs of their excited happiness in anticipating a fishing trip:

> "And as for this Robert Cohn," Bill said, "he makes me sick, and he can go to hell, and I'm damn glad he's staying here so we won't have him fishing with us."
>
> "You're damn right."
>
> "We're going trout-fishing. We're going trout-fishing in the Irati River, and we're going to get tight now at lunch on the wine of the country, and then take a swell bus ride."
>
> "Come on. Let's go over to the Iruna and start," I said. (82)

But perhaps the most significant use of functional profanity in *The Sun Also Rises* occurs in its final pages after Jake arrives in Madrid to rescue Brett. When Jake received Brett's urgent call for help—

COULD YOU COME HOTEL MONTANA MADRID AM RATHER
IN TROUBLE BRETT

he became angry, as his profanity indicates: "Well, that meant San Sebastián all shot to hell" (192). He remained angry as his train to Madrid passes an historical site and he "did not give a damn about it" (193). But once in Madrid with Brett, first at her hotel room, then at the bar of the Palace Hotel, followed by lunch at Botin's restaurant and then a carriage ride on Madrid's Gran Via, Jake uses profanity only once, not in the heat of emotion but as an intensifier to buoy Brett's sagging spirit: "You were probably damn good for him" (194). By contrast, Brett swears eleven times—a crucial sign of her emotional turmoil after Romero left her alone, friendless and penniless, in an unfamiliar city. Although Brett tells Jake that she made Romero "go" (194), everything we learn suggests that it was Romero who chose to leave Brett (see Daiker, "Brett Couldn't Hold Him"). So perhaps for the first time in her life, Brett has been dumped by a man. No wonder she feels so bad. No wonder she cries and shakes. No wonder she will not look directly at Jake. Brett wants to "feel rather good … feel rather set up" (195), but she can't pull it off: "Then I saw that she was crying. I could feel her crying. Shaking and crying. She wouldn't look up" (195). Brett is in the depths of despair and self-hatred when she says, "I'm going back to Mike…. He's so damned nice and he's so awful. He's my sort of thing" (195), echoing the bullfighter Belmonte's dismissal of his rival Marcial as "the sort of thing he knew all about" (172). But even after this admission, Brett cannot stop talking about Romero. "How can I help it," she woefully asks Jake (197).

The final instance of functional profanity in *The Sun Also Rises* is a negative one. Hemingway changed the original last line of the novel from Jake's "It's nice as hell to think so" (Facsimile 616) to "Isn't it pretty to think so?" so as not to let the profanity suggest that Jake is angry or upset. Hemingway's transforming Jake's "nice as hell" to "pretty"—along with his recasting Jake's statement as a question—shows Jake in complete emotional control of his relationship with Brett. That "pretty" is to be taken ironically is confirmed by its earlier usage: after Mike has hurled insults at Romero and then tried to attack Cohn, Brett asks, "Hasn't he [Michael] been pretty?" (145). Jake's emotional equilibrium, underscored by his not swearing, contrasts with Brett's agitation as she tries to get over Romero's rejection by embracing the illusion of a "damned good time" (198) with Jake.

"It is not about sex"—Ernest Hemingway

There is no denying its sexual themes, but to claim that *Sun* focuses on adultery and sexuality is to miss the heart of the novel. There is adultery, of course, but not much and then only if we assume that Lady Brett's unhappy marriage to the deranged Lord Ashley is still recognized. Brett characterizes her three-week tryst with Cohn in San Sebastián as dull and "Not frightfully amusing" rather than exciting and arousing (62). For her, "it didn't mean anything" (145). Brett's three lovers—Robert Cohn, her fiancé Mike Campbell, and Pedro Romero—are all unmarried. And all three affairs end badly. The last we see of Robert Cohn he is crying, self-pitying, and asking Jake to forgive him because "I've been through hell, Jake. It's been simply hell" (155). For Brett, she is relieved to be rid of "that damned Cohn" (195). Mike Campbell, an undischarged bankrupt, is last seen unable to pay his bar bill and unsure if Brett will ever return to him. Brett herself, "rather in trouble" (192) in Madrid because Romero has abandoned her there (see Daiker "Brett Couldn't Hold Him"), is "Shaking and crying" as she begs Jake, "Please don't let's ever talk about it" (195). Adultery proves to be bad news all around.

Sexuality appears briefly—and comically—in a scene in a Paris nightclub when gay men take turns dancing with the sex worker Georgette. "I do declare," a gay man calls to his friend Lett, "There is an actual harlot. I'm going to dance with her…. You watch me" (17). Hemingway's playful attitude toward sexuality is further manifest in a letter to the Canadian writer Morley Callaghan: "All the women in the novel get screwed with the exception of a girl called Edna who is not in the story long enough." Then Hemingway asserted, in a more serious vein, that the novel "is not about sex" (*Letters* 112). But sexuality—or its absence—is crucial to the novel's central relationship between Jake Barnes and Lady Brett Ashley. Jake has been injured in World War I so that he and Brett are unable to physically consummate their love. But the fact that Jake Barnes cannot perform—Hemingway told interviewer George Plimpton that Jake "was capable of all normal feelings as a *man* but incapable of consummating them" (Plimpton 25)—is handled with such restraint and delicacy that many first-time readers miss it completely. Indeed, the scene in Jake's Paris apartment bedroom where the two try once again to achieve some satisfying form of sexual intimacy goes unrecognized even by so scrupulous a scholar as H. R. Stoneback. Aside from this one instance of frustrated sexuality, all love-making in *The Sun Also Rises* occurs far offstage.

Robert Cohn "had a hard, Jewish, stubborn streak"
—Jake Barnes

I believe that *The Sun Also Rises* is mildly anti-Semitic. Its one Jewish character— the American expatriate writer Robert Cohn—is the butt of jokes and is once called a "kike." But these slurs largely come not from Hemingway surrogate Jake Barnes but from the hard-drinking Bill Gorton and the drunkard Mike Campbell. Jake makes only a single anti-Semitic comment, and it is something he thinks but does not say; it occurs early in the novel in response to Robert's obsession to travel to South America: "He had a hard, Jewish, stubborn streak" (9). Jake never utters an anti-Semitic comment out loud. The few remaining anti-Semitic slurs come from others: Brett, Mike, and especially Bill. Brett's one anti-Semitic slur occurs as part of her effort to justify her lust for Romero. "What do you think it's meant to have that damn Jew about?" (147), she pleads to Jake. Mike's first slur occurs when he urges Cohn to "Go away. Go away for God's sake. Take that sad Jewish face away" (142). But this is the only point in the novel when Cohn hears an anti-Semitic comment; he is not "taunt[ed] with antisemitic remarks" by "the others," as has been claimed ("The Sun Also Rises"). Later, inebriated, Mike summarizes what the fiesta has meant for him: "Brett's got a bull-fighter.... But her Jew has gone away" (168).

Bill's anti-Semitism is more frequent and more serious, part of the same impulse that leads him to threaten to "join the Klan" (71). When Cohn lies about his relationship with Brett, Bill asks Jake, "Haven't you got some more Jewish friends you could bring along?" (81). Bill later charges Cohn with "Jewish superiority so strong that he thinks the only emotion he'll get out of the [bull]fight will be being bored" (130). At the fight itself when Jake asks if Cohn looks bored, Bill responds with the most virulent insult in the novel: "That kike!" (131).[2] But Jake never reinforces or echoes Bill's insults; he either changes the subject or remains silent. Ironically, it is Bill who seems to take Cohn's part after Cohn has knocked out Jake and savagely beaten Romero; it is Bill who urges Jake to see Cohn, who's "been in a jam" that's left him "in bad shape" (154).

But the novel's mild anti-Semitism disappears completely and permanently in its last two chapters: there is not a single anti-Semitic note during the last day of the fiesta or during the closing scenes in Pamplona, Bayonne, San Sebastián, or Madrid. In fact, Cohn's final act in the novel is one of understanding and empathy: after pleading for and receiving Jake's forgiveness, he asks his dazed friend, "Are you all right, Jake?" (155). Then, true to his word, Cohn leaves Pamplona without incident and with all bills paid. The novel's final reference to Jews seems to undercut stereotypical charges of greed and avarice: Mike tells Jake that Brett pays most of her yearly allowance "to Jews." But then Mike clarifies his statement: "They're not really Jews. We just call them Jews. They're Scotsmen, I believe" (185). Hemingway's point is clear: Jews, like Cohn, are often scapegoats, wrongly blamed for what others have done.

"a jazz superficial story"

On top of charges of profanity, obscenity, and anti-Semitism, *The Sun Also Rises* has often been labeled as trivial, as superficial, as lacking seriousness and devoid of redeeming social value. Some early critics, while not calling for the novel's outright banning, suggested that the work simply be ignored. Contemporary reviews frequently found the novel pointless and even frivolous. The earliest review, in the *Cincinnati Enquirer*, characterizes *The Sun Also Rises* as "a book, which, like its characters, begins nowhere and ends in nothing" (Stephens 31), anticipating critic Philip Young's assertion that the novel presents "motion which goes no place" (57). A contemporaneous reviewer for *Dial* magazine wrote that Hemingway's "characters are as shallow as the saucers in which they stack their daily emotions …" (Stephens 43). The reviewer for the *Chicago Daily Tribune* called the novel "a bushel of sensationalism and triviality" (Stephens 39). Even Hemingway's friend and fellow writer John Dos Passos piled on; he mocked *Sun* as "a cock and bull story about a lot of summer tourists getting drunk and making fools of themselves at a picturesque Italian folk-festival" (*Letters* 184–85). Hemingway's London publisher Jonathan Cape understood the novel as less than serious, titling it not *The Sun Also Rises* but *Fiesta*, and advertising it as "an amusing story of the sort of thing young Americans are doing in the Latin quarter today" as if it were a "hammock book" (*Letters* 251). Hemingway was surprised, disappointed, and even "disgusted" (*Letters* 252) by such characterizations. Not in any way a hammock book, Hemingway told Fitzgerald that *Sun* "is such a hell of a sad story—and not one at all for children to read" (*Letters* 75). "It's funny," Hemingway wrote to Perkins, "to write a book that seems as tragic as that and have them take it as a jazz superficial story. If you went any deeper inside they couldn't read it because they would be crying all the time" (*Letters* 148).

The dismissals of *Sun* as shallow and superficial were especially galling to Hemingway because he had worked so hard writing and revising it. In contrast to his light satire *Torrents of Spring*, which he claimed to have written in ten days (*Letters* 22), he labored tirelessly over *Sun*, "working and reworking" the manuscript, "three times re-writing" it (*Letters* 112). In *A Moveable Feast*, Hemingway's memoir of his Paris days in the 1920s, he wrote that reworking *Sun* was "the most difficult job of rewriting that I have ever done … when I had to take the first draft of *The Sun Also Rises* which I had written in one sprint of six weeks, and make it into a novel" (202). Even after Hemingway had sent off the completed typescript of *Sun* to Perkins, he knew he wasn't finished with his novel, telling Perkins that he planned to "do additional working over in the proofs" (*Letters* 64).

Modern criticism has come to acknowledge the importance and achievement of *The Sun Also Rises*, in part through recognition of the novel's complexity. "*The Sun Also Rises* is a difficult book to read correctly," Linda W. Wagner has written, "until the reader understands the way it works; then it becomes a masterpiece of concentration, with every detail conveying multiple impressions, and every speech creating character and complex relationships" (98). The editors of the Hemingway Letter Project recognize it as "one of the signature works of the twentieth century" (*Letters* xvi). Stoneback regards the work as "one of the most important twentieth-century American novels …," and as a "masterpiece of modernism" that "stands at the center of Hemingway's artistic vision …" (xi). But it is more than recognition of complexity that has elevated *Sun* to the highest levels of praise; it is also its richness and depth. Critical studies have explored in detail the novel's relationship to the wasteland theme, the contrast between France and Spain as metaphor, the richness of the brief San Sebastián episode (Knodt, Vopat), the intricate dialogue between Jake and Brett in the novel's final scene, its "morality of compensation" (Donaldson), and the symbolic significance of bullfighting in general and of Pedro Romero in particular (Ganzel, Josephs): standing in the center of the ring, all alone, the torero faces and defeats the murderous force charging him. For Romero, it's a bull named Bocanegra; for us, that murderous force might be unrequited love, betrayal, divorce, drug or alcohol addiction, bankruptcy, job loss, the death of a parent, the loss of a child, or the banning of one's beloved book. In living his life "all the way up" (9), the true bullfighter—Romero is "a real one" (131)—provides a model of confronting and surmounting whatever threatens to overwhelm us.

Hemingway was fully aware of efforts to ban books like his. In 1923, 1924, and 1925 a Clean Books League bill was proposed to the New York state legislature by John S. Sumner of the New York Society for the Suppression of Vice and by New York Supreme Court Justice John Ford. But Hemingway obviously did not take their efforts seriously, closing a 1926 letter to F. Scott Fitzgerald with "Always your co-worker for the Clean Books Bill" and signing it as "Ernest M. Shit" (*Letters* 76–77).

Miami University

Notes

1. All references to *The Sun Also Rises* are to the Hemingway Library Edition.

2. Hemingway's March 5, 1927, letter to his friend Isabelle Simmons Godolphin begins, "Dearest Izz: I certainly have been a kike bastard not to have written …" (*Letters* 214).

Works Cited

"Bannings and Burnings in History." *Freedom to Read*, www.freedomtoread.ca/resources/bannings-and-burnings-in-history/.

Bruccoli, Matthew J., editor. *The Only Thing That Counts: The Hemingway/Maxwell Perkins Correspondence, 1925–1947*. Scribner, 1996.

Daiker, Donald A. "'Brett Couldn't Hold Him': Lady Ashley, Pedro Romero, and the Madrid Sequence of *The Sun Also Rises*." *The Hemingway Review*, vol. 29, no. 1, fall 2009, pp. 73–86.

Donaldson, Scott. "Hemingway's Morality of Compensation." *American Literature*, vol. 43, no. 3, Nov. 1971, pp. 399–420.

Ganzel, Dewey. "*Cabestro* and *Vaquilla*: The Symbolic Structure of *The Sun Also Rises*." *The Sewanee Review*, vol. 76, no. 1, winter 1968, pp. 26–48.

Hemingway, Ernest. *The Letters of Ernest Hemingway. Vol. 3. 1926–1929*. Edited by Rena Sanderson, Sandra Spanier, and Robert W. Trogdon, Cambridge UP, 2015.

———. *A Moveable Feast*. Scribners, 1964.

———. *The Sun Also Rises*. Facsimile Edition. Parts One and Two. Edited by Matthew J. Bruccoli, Omnigraphics, 1990.

———. *The Sun Also Rises*. Hemingway Library Edition, Scribners, 2014.

Hemingway, Grace Hall. "ALS Gracie 4 Dec 1926, Oak Park, IL, 6pp., w/newspaper clipping and envelope." Ernest Hemingway Personal Papers, John F. Kennedy Presidential Library and Museum, Boston, box IC11, folder: Hemingway, Grace Hall, 1920–1927.

Josephs, Allen. "*Toreo*: the Moral Axis of *The Sun Also Rises*." *The Hemingway Review*, vol. 6, no. 1, fall 1986, pp. 88–99.

Knodt, Ellen Andrews. "Diving Deep: Jake's Moment of Truth at San Sebastián." *The Hemingway Review*, vol. 17, no. 1, fall 1997, pp. 28–37.

Pendharkar, Eesha. "Who's Behind the Escalating Push to Ban Books? A New Report Has Answers." *Education Week*, 19 Sept. 2022, updated 28 Sept. 2022. www.edweek.org/leadership/whos-behind-the-escalating-push-to-ban-books-a-new-report-has-answers/2022/09.

Plimpton, George. "An Interview with Ernest Hemingway." *Ernest Hemingway's* The Sun Also Rises: *A Casebook*, edited by Linda Wagner-Martin, Oxford UP, 2002, pp. 15–32.

Stephens, Robert O., editor. *Ernest Hemingway: The Critical Reception*. Burt Franklin, 1977.

Stoneback, H. R. *Reading Hemingway's* The Sun Also Rises: *Glossary and Commentary*. Kent State UP, 2007.

"The Sun Also Rises." *Wikipedia*, en.wikipedia.org/wiki/The_Sun_Also_Rises.

Wagner, Linda W. "*The Sun Also Rises*: One Debt to Imagism." *The Journal of Narrative Theory*, vol. 2, no. 2, May 1972, pp. 88–98.

Vopat, Carole Gottlieb. "The End of *The Sun Also Rises*: A New Beginning." 1972. Reprinted in *Brett Ashley*, edited by Harold Bloom, Chelsea House, 1991, pp, 96–104. Major Literary Characters.

Young, Philip. *Ernest Hemingway*. Rinehart, 1952.

AVOIDING THE "WEATHERING" OF BLACK GIRLS BY NOT BANNING TONI MORRISON'S *THE BLUEST EYE*

Marilyn Judith Atlas

Reading about the culture of others can help us understand the diverse world we live in and how to improve it, and thereby help to improve our well-being and extend our lives. University of Michigan Public Health researcher Arline T. Geronimus recently wrote a book about racial health inequities in the United States and how unfair treatment degrades the bodies of marginalized people, "weathers" them. In this over 300-page book, *Weathering: The Extraordinary Stress of Ordinary Life in an Unjust Society*, she gives readers the facts: marginalized Americans are disproportionately more likely to suffer from chronic illness and to die at much younger ages. Black people experience early health decline as a consequence of environmental stressors—social, economic, and political. Black women are more likely to have hypertensive disorders, fertility issues, higher risk of breast cancer and breast cancer deaths, difficult pregnancies, and poor birth outcomes, which increase with maternal age. The childbirth death rate for Black mothers is three times higher than for white mothers. In her book, Geronimus theorizes and demonstrates that injustice erodes the health of marginalized people, men and women. Geronimus documents that stress, even the stress of playing by the rules, leaves markers on the human biological canvas, and the distressed genes and cells are more quickly weathered. "Do nothing about us without us" (Geronimus 256), Geronimus also reminds readers: minorities must speak in their own words and for themselves and those less marginalized must listen. She coined the term "weathering" to describe the effects of systemic oppression, and throughout this book she insists that we ask ourselves why Black people weather more quickly than white people. She repeatedly answers her own question: social injustice is the culprit, and it particularly marks Black bodies in a racist culture.

Toni Morrison in her first novel, *The Bluest Eye* (1970), creates weathered characters and demonstrates that this weathering marks their bodies: Cholly Breedlove dies young; Pecola loses her baby as well as her mind; Marie, or, The Maginot Line, a sex worker more powerless than Poland during World War II, is obese, probably a sign of weathering; and Polly Breedlove loses her front tooth when chewing candy, a tooth perhaps invisibly damaged by relentless, continuous stress that she experiences throughout her lonely life. One way to curb the effects of sexist, racist, and classist oppression is by reading books such as Toni Morrison's *The Bluest Eye*, yet, ironically, according to the American Library Association's Advocacy, Legislation & Issues website, this book was challenged 73 times in 2022 and is the third most banned book in 2022 ("Top 13 Most Challenged"). By understanding a novel that in Morrison's words "pecks away at the gaze that condemns her" (Foreword xi) girls like Pecola Breedlove can come to understand that "Beauty was not simply something to behold; it was something one could *do*" (Foreword xi, italics in original). Reading this novel might literally help to stop some of the damage done to Black girls living in a racist society by giving them insight and a few tools to fight against low self-esteem, to recognize bullying, injustice, and internalized oppression, and thereby, through reading, to slow down the effects of weathering.

Morrison wrote this novel because she needed to read it. In her article "Invisible Ink: Reading the Writing and Writing the Reading," she stresses the value of reading: "Reading is fundamental—emphasis on the 'fun.' At the least, of course, it is understood, in popular discourse, to be uplifting, instructive; at its best encouraging deep thought" (346). It is therefore particularly troubling that "Parental Rights" groups and legislators who say they mean to protect our children are doing the exact opposite in banning a book by a Nobel- and Pulitzer Prize–winning minority writer, a book that could help inspire adolescents to resist oppression, to love themselves, and to learn to write their own stories. All people need to see people like themselves in books. If one wants to better understand minority experiences and positions, one must study the writings of minority authors. Audre Lorde reminds us in *Sister Outsider* that the master's tools will never dismantle the master's house" (Lorde 110). In *The Bluest Eye* Claudia MacTeer, the narrator of the novel, speaks for herself and explains midwestern life in Lorain, Ohio, and what she experienced in 1940–41 when she was nine years old and her friend and neighbor, Pecola Breedlove, was impregnated by her broken father, Cholly Breedlove, a man who had experienced forced, humiliating sex as a teen and who never recovered from it. Morrison explains her understanding of Cholly Breedlove in her foreword to the 1993 Knopf edition of the *The Bluest Eye*:

> I knew that some victims of powerful self-loathing turn out to be dangerous, violent, reproducing the enemy who has humiliated them over and over. Others surrender their identity; melt into a structure that delivers the strong persona they lack. Most others, however, grow beyond it. But there are some who collapse, silently, anonymously, with no voice to express or acknowledge it. They are invisible. The death of self-esteem can occur quickly, easily in children, before their ego has 'legs,' so to speak. Couple the vulnerability of youth with indifferent parents, dismissive adults, and a world, which, in its language, laws and images, re-enforces despair and the journey to destruction is sealed. (Foreword ix–x)

If "Parental Rights" groups want to help their children understand oppression and to live in and create a more just and healthier world for all, they need to let educators teach books like *The Bluest Eye*, and they need to make sure public libraries have multiple copies to loan out to their readers who are trying to understand the world and find their way. Morrison, through her honest, resistant narrator, Claudia MacTeer, has much to teach readers about midwestern life in 1941, about Black Americans, some transports from the South, as well as other ethnic groups living in Lorain, Ohio, as she tries to understand their power, pain, poverty, problems, and choices, and she has much to share with readers about the cost of living in a world where Black lives do not matter enough, and where the not-so-subtle messages of hegemony and entitlement poison hearts that, like all hearts, deserve to sing and thrive.

According to Alisha Haridasani Gupta's *New York Times* article, "How 'Weathering' Contributes to Racial Disparities," in 1990 Dr. Arline Geronimus first introduced the term "weathering," but that term and her theory about the cost of oppression was, until recently, largely ignored. Geronimus has theorized and scientifically demonstrated that young Black women have better pregnancy outcomes in their late teens than in their mid-twenties when racism has already taken its toll. Geronimus posits and alerts the public that generalized health recommendations can be detrimental to minorities and that what is good for comparatively "unweathered" white women can be harmful to oppressed Black women. What better way to understand the experiences of Black girls than by reading and analyzing books written by Toni Morrison, a socially conscious Black award-winning writer?

Besides her best-known honors, the Pulitzer Prize and the Nobel Prize, Toni Morrison has won many other awards, among them the Ohioana Book Award, the National Book Critics Circle Award, The American Book Award, and the Library of Congress Creative Achievement Award for Fiction. In 2012 President Barack Obama recognized her achievements by awarding her the Medal of Freedom and in 2020 Juda Bennett, Winnifred Brown-Glaude, Cassandra Jackson, and Piper Kendrix Williams formed a reading community and wrote a book, *The Toni Morrison Book Club*, and prefaced it with an epigraph from the remarks given by the person who introduced Morrison's 1993 Nobel Prize lecture in literature, remarks that demonstrated how powerful and memorable an artist Toni Morrison was and is: "Her reputation for wisdom is without peer and without question. Among her people she is both the law and its transgression" (qtd. in Bennett et al. i). And yet this brilliant writer is among the most banned authors in America, and *The Bluest Eye* one of the most banned books.

Morrison's are not the only books banned. The American Library Association's Office for Intellectual Freedom, in its March 2023 report, disclosed that in 2022 it counted close to 1,300 attempts to restrict library books and resources in the United States and added that since these types of statistics began being recorded over 20 years ago, this was their highest count ever (Garcia). On May 9, 2023, *The New York Times* printed part of a podcast conversation in reaction to this increasingly frequent attempt to limit book access. The conversation was between Gilbert Cruz, editor of *The New York Times Book Review* and host of "The Book Review Podcast," and two reporters, Alexandra Alter and Elizabeth Harris, who cover the publishing industry. These three alerted the nation that prize-winning books such as Toni Morrison's *The Bluest Eye* were under attack. This novel has been faulted for equality, diversity, and inclusive content, as if that were a fault, and its critics claim the novel depicts sexually explicit material (which it does not), and explores incest and child abuse, and therefore should be banned from public schools and libraries (Alter, Cruz, and Harris). The picture associated with this article/book banning conversation illustrates this: out of the thirty plus banned books depicted in the photograph, five of them are written by Toni Morrison. Some of the book titles and authors are purposefully blurred in the photograph accompanying the article, but readers can clearly see *The Bluest Eye*, perhaps multiple copies of it, and *Paradise* among the three stacks of books. "Parental Rights" organizations, Alter, Cruz, and Harris explain, want this book to be made as inaccessible as possible. The message of this *New York Times* article is to inform the public that this type of book banning is on the rise, is dangerous, and that this disturbing trend must be faced and reversed before it does more harm. Banning books such as *The Bluest Eye* is detrimental to the well-being of Black girls who, in order to be mentally and physically healthy, need to read material written by writers like themselves and diverse writers, books that will help them to understand the world and create for themselves a good place in it.

Book banning is not a midwestern phenomenon, but it exists in this region as well as nationally. Recently, thankfully, Midwest library book bans put in place in states like Iowa are being reversed. Judge Stephen Locher on Friday, December 29, 2023, blocked Iowa's ban on certain library books. The Republican Legislature banned books describing "sex acts" from public school libraries. According to *New York Times* reporter Mitch Smith, Locher temporarily blocked the injunction stating that the law, "makes no attempt to target such books in any reasonable way …" (17). According to Smith, Locher wrote, "The underlying message is that there is no redeeming value to any such book even if it is a work of history, a self-help guide, award-winning novel or other piece of serious literature. In effect, the Legislature has imposed a puritanical 'pall of orthodoxy' over school libraries" (Smith 17). Iowa is not alone in changing course nor the first to do so.

A year earlier, teenagers in St. Louis, Missouri, also had *The Bluest Eye* banned from their school and public libraries and then that ban was also rescinded, and young people were once again able to find *The Bluest Eye* on their school and library shelves. A web article celebrates the reversal and the attention that 2022 reversal received: "The Wentzville School District Board of Education held a special meeting Friday afternoon to vote on rescinding the ban on the book. The district made national news last month when it voted to remove the book from its library" (Stegan).

In June 2023 there was also good news forbidding the banning of books: in Illinois book bans were banned. Governor J. B. Pritzker had the correct idea—he used government not to legislate the banning of books but to legislate the illegality of banning them in Illinois. On June 12, 2023, Illinois became the first state in the nation to prohibit book bans (Yip and Chavez). Governor Pritzker was among the first to understand that banning books was absurd and he had the foresight and power to do something about it. In a press release Governor Pritzker is quoted:

> "Here in Illinois, we don't hide from the truth, we embrace it … Young people shouldn't be kept from learning about the realities of our world; I want them to become critical thinkers, exposed to ideas that they disagree with, proud of what our nation has overcome, and thoughtful about what comes next. Everyone deserves to see themselves reflected in the books they read, the art they see, the history they learn. In Illinois, we are showing the nation what it really looks like to stand up for liberty." ("Gov. Pritzker")

How better to combat "weathering" for minority girls than to give them access to books like Toni Morrison's *The Bluest Eye* and to read and analyze these books together with other students in a classroom?

In the December 11, 2023, issue of *The Columbus Dispatch* Stephan Pastis's comic strip "Pearls Before Swine" demonstrates that even the writers of comic strips are joining the conversation. In the first of the strip's three frames, Goat, the long-suffering philosopher who spends his days trying to comprehend the perplexities of existence, is sitting at his table peacefully humming while sipping his morning coffee. There are no words in this frame. In the second frame another character, Rat, an often arrogant and cynical know-it-all, uses a megaphone to interrupt his friend's morning coffee with the following words in the form of an announcement: "I INTERRUPT YOUR COFFEE WITH A SOLUTION TO BOOK BANNING. IT'S CALLED, 'IF YOU DON'T LIKE THE BOOK, JUST DON'T BUY IT.'" In this second frame Goat jumps up from his chair because Rat's announcement is so loud, and in the third frame, as Goat falls off his chair, he asks Rat, "IS THE MEGAPHONE NECESSARY?" and Goat responds, still through the megaphone, "GENIUS IDEAS NEED MEGAPHONES!" (Pastis).

This laugh-out-loud cartoon demonstrates that thinking about book banning has entered the everyday life of midwesterners from courts to comics. The strip is simultaneously funny and serious: why do some individuals need to control what librarians and teachers should be controlling? What gives these individuals the authority and permission to limit access and discourage public school, teenage readers from reading prize-winning authors such as Toni Morrison?

If a book such as Toni Morrison's *The Bluest Eye* is banned from schools and libraries, all students will lose. But particularly Black girls will suffer. Banning this book is dangerous because it deprives our most vulnerable youth easy access to a well-crafted work of art that explores racism, sexism, class, caste, and innate goodness. Understanding Blackness can curb the ill effects of systemic injustice.

Geronimus, in her book, *Weathering*, wants her readers to find a way forward out of this evil destruction. One chapter, "Think Biopsychosocially: Address the Stealth Inequities That Surround Us" (Geronimus 229–50) attempts to help readers figure out ways to rectify these evils and improve Black lives. How better to address the stealth inequities than by encouraging the reading of a novel that directly addresses stealth inequities?

If you ban Toni Morrison's *The Bluest Eye*, you encourage young Black people to miss an opportunity to read about people who look like them, to see how racism can twist and shorten lives, and how culturally imposed self-hate can affect young people, particularly Black girls who feel and believe that to deserve love they must be beautiful and to be beautiful one must be white, ideally with blue eyes. Mainstream culture offers Black girls and women a ridiculous and destructive beauty standard that one must fight against in order for Black women and girls to be happy and healthy. For Black girls with dark eyes this standard is unattainable and amounts to internalized hate and early, unnecessary weathering. Reading *The Bluest Eye* can help young Black women understand and resist racist popular culture's beauty standards, and by understanding it become more equipped to fight it and be less weathered by it. In sum, artificial, imposed, distorted, and inaccurate definitions are marketed to the most vulnerable on what is and what is not beautiful, and *The Bluest Eye* provides an antidote to this poison.

Banning books exacerbates the problem of racism, classism, caste, and gender in America. *The Bluest Eye* has much to teach readers about the cost of living in a world where Black lives don't matter enough and where Black people, particularly Black girls and women, identify too frequently and too much with those in power. The beauty standard of 1941 when the novel takes place, the beauty standard in 1970 when the novel is published, and the beauty standard today harm girls and women. These girls learn to prefer blue eyes to darker ones, and they learn not to like themselves. They learn to feel that they are genetically "less than" and that nothing short of a miracle will make them good enough for love when in reality they are beautiful and nothing is wrong with them; rather, something is very wrong with a culture where oppression, inequity, and inequality are normative and where students do not have easy access to books that can foster better, life-affirming perspectives.

We can use, and should use, and do use Toni Morrison's *The Bluest Eye* to help girls gain perspective as they attempt to weather the storms that they will inevitably face in a sexist and racist society. Frieda MacTeer, in loving Shirley Temple, will pay a price in loving her because, being Black, she cannot be like her, just as her younger sister, Claudia MacTeer, in not loving Shirley Temple will pay a price of resistance, of owning her difference. Resistance isn't free but resistance is worth it. Claudia learns to analyze, to question, to describe, and she never stops feeling. She holds her ground in a positive way.

Claudia demonstrates that she has an innate sense of justice, what Frans de Waal describes so well in *The Bonobo and the Atheist: In Search of Humanism Among the Primates*. One does not need G-d in order to understand morality. De Waal explains,

> Perhaps it's just me, but I am wary of any persons whose belief system is the only thing standing between them and repulsive behavior. Why not assume that our humanity, including the self-control needed for a livable society, is built into us? Does anyone truly believe that our ancestors lacked social norms before they had religion? Did they never assist others in need, or complain about an unfair deal? Humans must have worried about the functioning of their communities well before current religions arose, which occurred only a couple of millennia ago. (2–3)

Many characters in *The Bluest Eye* demonstrate this sense of caring and this sense of justice. China, Poland, and Marie, the Maginot Line, three sex workers, live upstairs from Pecola and care about her. They tease her and keep her company as they amuse themselves with banter. The narrator explains,

> Three merry gargoyles. Three merry harridans. Amused by a long-ago time of ignorance. They did not belong to those generations of prostitutes created in novels, with great and generous hearts, dedicated, because of the horror of circumstance, to ameliorating the luckless, barren life of men, taking money incidentally and humbly for their "understanding." Nor were they from that sensitive breed of young girl, gone wrong at the hands of fate.... Neither were they the sloppy, inadequate whores who, unable to make a living at it alone, turn to drug consumption and traffic or pimps to help complete their scheme of self-destruction, avoiding suicide only to punish the memory of some absent father or to sustain the misery of some silent mother. Except for Marie's fabled love for Dewey Prince, these women hated men, all men, without shame, apology, or discrimination.... all

were inadequate and weak … and were the recipients of their disinterested wrath. (55–56)

Morrison is funny, realistic, astute, and readers come to understand that to see accurately and understand, one must look and not simply make things up. Marie, the Maginot Line, was not simply one thing. She could entertain Pecola, and she could punish the snobbishness of the MacTeer girls. She threw an empty brown glass root beer bottle at Frieda and Claudia because these girls were obeying their mom and refusing to enter the Maginot Line's apartment or use her plates or utensils. When they refuse her offer of a place to wait for their friend, Pecola Breedlove, and some "pop" to drink (103), Frieda explains to Marie that her mother would not allow this simple, civil interaction because as Frieda understood the problem, their mom did not want them to be "ruined" (101). Marie understands and is angry. Silently, she finishes drinking a bottle of root beer on her porch. She seems to know exactly what she is doing, and where she is aiming, when she tosses the bottle over the rail at the girls' feet. The bottle splits at their feet and "shards of brown glass dappled" their legs before they "jumped back" (104). Frieda is surprised and frightened. She fears her mother's wrath because she conversed with Marie, but she also fears her "terrible" laugh, a laugh that she does not understand. Claudia is younger and, in this instance, braver than her older by one year sister, Frieda. She refuses to be traumatized by her interaction with Marie. Claudia does not swerve and is still determined to find Pecola, even if it means going to the Lake District. She and her sister can look at the homes that fill that white and affluent suburb, even if she and her sister can only dream of using the parks. In 1941 Black people were not allowed to enter these parks (105), except in their dreams and so they dreamed and were weathered by the racism that ran and runs the United States.

One can grow as a reader and a person experiencing the pain and the beauty of the lakefront houses and Mrs. Breedlove's mistreatment of Pecola and her friends when Frieda and Claudia arrive at Mrs. Breedlove's place of employment. Mrs. Breedlove, housekeeper and nanny, is kind only to the little white girl in pink and soothes her. She is not kind to her own daughter, punishing Pecola for accidentally dropping a hot pie and accidentally sullying a spotless floor:

> In one gallop she was on Pecola, and with the back of her hand knocked her to the floor. Pecola slid in the pie juice, one leg folding under her. Mrs. Breedlove yanked her up by the arm, slapped her again, and in a voice thin with anger, abused Pecola directly and Frieda and me by implication.... and we backed away in dread. (109)

This time, as opposed to the earlier scene with Marie, Claudia, as well as Frieda, is traumatized: in this scene Mrs. Breedlove's words are "hotter and darker than the smoking berries" (109). Did Marie scare her less, although she threw a brown glass bottle at her feet and laughed an incomprehensible laugh because somehow this was worse, an unjustified anger that showed her feelings mattered so much less than a little white girl's feelings? Mrs. Breedlove's language is cruel and brutal, "Crazy fool ... my floor, mess ... look what you ... work ... get out ... now that ... crazy ... my floor, my floor ... my floor" (109). This is not Mrs. Breedlove's home; this is not her floor; this is her daughter and her daughter's friends she is abusing. Mrs. Breedlove spits out words "like rotten pieces of apple" (109). Is Morrison giving the reader a domestic fruit pie image or one of Adam and Eve's fall from the Garden of Eden? Does a Black mother damage her daughter and her daughter's friends more than any harlot ever could?

One doesn't blame Mrs. Breedlove because we know she, like her daughter, is broken. Polly was a lonely child, too much alone, someone who loved order and beauty and wanted to be saved by a prince. Instead, she married a broken man, Cholly, a rejected orphan, a victim of sexual abuse, a humiliated man who searched for his father only to meet rejection, a man who becomes an alcoholic and rapes his own daughter at least twice. For Mrs. Breedlove who loved the movies and thought herself ugly, her white employer's home is her last escape from an unjust and humiliating world, only slightly more realistic as an escape than her daughter's fantasized and most beautiful blue eyes. The beauty myth, white America's love affair with itself, helps to destroy both mother and daughter. Little girls don't outgrow the effects of self-loathing and this self-loathing weathers and breaks both mother and daughter, in many ways mirrors of one another. The pain in this relationship is palpable and the reader feels terrible sadness for a world that allows a mother to betray her own and embrace a world that will use her up, spit her out, and drive her daughter mad.

It is Pecola who needs and deserves her mom's hugs, but Mrs. Breedlove has entered a world where only her rich, white employer's daughter matters. The reader feels the perversity and the tragedy and we experience the twistedness of Mrs. Breedlove's displaced love, realizing that she is broken and by her cruelty toward Pecola almost guarantees that Pecola will be weathered beyond repair. Every child needs and deserves love. Pecola has none: her mother does not have the ability to love a little Black girl she has birthed and who she decides is ugly, just as she determines that she herself is unredeemably ugly. Cholly Breedlove's twisted, inappropriate, incestuous love irreparably harms Pecola, shaming and impregnating her, but perhaps no more than her mother's turning away from her toward a rich, beautifully dressed white girl, a girl with whom she can never compete in the real world.

Lisa Long theorizes that in this novel Morrison is asking readers to see the Midwest through the lens of Blackness rather than the usual colonial, monolithic, white perspective. Morrison is refusing stereotypes of the Midwest: the world *The Bluest Eye* creates is not fertile and it is not white. In 1941, Lorain, Ohio, is ethnic, filled with Black southern transplants like the Breedloves and the MacTeers who have come North in hope of creating a better life. Instead, they find racism, inequity, harsh weather, and decay, a decay that they, like Mrs. Breedlove through the symbol of her tooth, may have brought from the South, an invisible decay that ruins Mrs. Breedlove's hope for a future filled with beauty, wealth, romance, and transcendence. At two years old, Polly Breedlove's weathering began in Alabama with a nail that entered her foot. Lorain is a colorful but lonely place for her, a young, Black woman coming from Alabama and Kentucky and who has little understanding of a more urban, midwestern space. Some individuals weather the Midwest a great deal better than others—partially because they come to Lorain, Ohio, with different levels of trauma. Long explains,

> Reading *The Bluest Eye* as a prototypical Midwestern novel, then, illuminates the region's diasporic specificity and historical scope, helping explain how the region is understood as being both at the center of national life and on its margins. Such an approach recasts Midwesternism as not just shared setting or source of inspiration, but also, as a way of reading highly attuned to material details and it firmly situates African American culture in the geographical and historical space of the Midwest.... in *The Bluest Eye* she [Morrison] creates a less sanitized, but more worldly and inclusive view of the Midwest that hews closely to its historical roots. And from this standpoint, Pecola Breedlove emerges as a new kind of Midwestern protagonist who begets an alternative literary lineage. (105–06)

Lisa Long explains that what Morrison is creating in this novel has not existed before, a Black perspective that examines what it is like to live in racist Lorain, Ohio, for three young girls, particularly for Pecola, who simply cannot handle the cards she is dealt by a weathered and dysfunctional family and a racist culture. Claudia, Frieda, and Pecola teach readers what the Dick and Jane readers cannot: if they are Black, the world of Dick and Jane is not and cannot be their world. *The Bluest Eye*, unlike the Dick and Jane readers, makes room for Black lives and difficult lives. In this world of *The Bluest Eye*, Black and ethnic characters are not well, but neither are they invisible. Knowledge is power, and banning the study of a novel written by a brilliant Black writer is a cruel and damaging mistake.

In her foreword, Morrison states that in this novel she wanted to explore the "tragic and disabling consequences of accepting rejection as legitimate, as self-evident" (ix), and she does just that. And our public school students should have the right to easily access a novel written to help them negotiate the world so many of them live in.

Hegemonic cultures like America's can be fluid. One can sometimes move up a ladder, move from poverty to middle class, from middle class to upper class. But individuals can get trapped on the bottom, particularly if they are minorities, and this entrapment, when there is no exit, is more similar to a "caste" than a class system. Cholly Breedlove is an example of an individual broken and hopeless and stuck on the bottom of what appears to be a caste system. He rapes his daughter because he can, rationalizing his behavior, at least twice caught in a moment, indifferent to the harm, to his survival or hers. One can learn from this that even harmed, there are some choices, at least sometimes, and they can be evil, and they can cause harm to your health. Some individuals have the strength and support to resist or slow down weathering—Claudia, her mom, her sister, and her dad all resist and hold on and stay lovingly together. The MacTeers fight against brokenness and abuse, and they do not murder dogs or throw empty root beer bottles at the feet of children. They set goals and limits and they work very hard and consistently and try to do good by helping a ward of the state, a lost and troubled girl like Pecola. Cholly Breedlove, Mrs. Breedlove, and Pecola are amazing characters, but they are not resilient like the MacTeers. The Breedloves give up; Cholly stops trying, reverting to alcohol and conflating love and sexual abuse; Pauline Breedlove gets caught up in order and beauty forgetting who, what is truly hers and who is worthy of love; Pecola is so caught up with having achieved beauty, or worthiness, in the form of blue eyes, she cannot think past her miraculous achievement, is frozen by it, and in her madness cannot conceive of having or needing more. Toni Morrison examines various entrapments without judging, just giving each character she creates a backstory that helps readers see how these characters came to be who they are and how they come to do what they do.

To protect our children, we must allow them to see the world, but guide them so that they will not be owned by it, particularly if the culture treats them as "less than." No one can rewrite their lineage, but Pecola tries by getting herself a pair of imaginary blue eyes. She is ashamed of who she is and in a just world, she obviously should not be. All eleven-year-old children should be hopeful in a realistic, sustainable way, but Pecola is too weathered, and she has no hope except for magical solutions to her culturally imposed beauty problem.

Black girls need to see characters like Geraldine and Junior and how being a snob has costs and does damage, to cats, and boys, and mothers. Not being allowed to play with other Black children who Geraldine deems not good enough for her son, Junior, twists him into a sadist.

Healthy minorities, even in a racist environment, need not torture the cat (Junior) or poison the dog (Soaphead Church). Life offers choices and Toni Morrison's *The Bluest Eye* demonstrates that even in a summer where marigolds won't grow, wisdom can. Claudia may not feel the hope at the end of her narrative, but the reader does. A bad year does not necessarily imply a bad lifetime. What *The Bluest Eye* teaches readers is to resist acceptance of inequity.

Isabel Wilkerson, in *Caste: The Origins of Our Discontents*, explains how she sees Indian untouchables and Black Americans as similarly entrapped—and that we can and must resist. She explains that Martin Luther King, Jr., when visiting India in 1959, eleven years before *The Bluest Eye* was published, found that the people of Bombay, Delhi, and even Trivandrum in the state of Kerala, had been following the trials of his own oppressed people in America and knew of the bus boycott he had led. He felt like a rock star in India because people sought his autograph. When visiting with high school students whose families had been untouchables, the principal introduced him in a way that he found shocking: "Young people," he said, "I would like to present to you a fellow untouchable from the United States of America" (Wilkerson 22–23). King was floored at first, but then he began to realize that the 20 million people consigned to the lowest rank in America for centuries, "still smothering in an airtight cage of poverty," quarantined in isolated ghettos, exiled in their own country, that, indeed, he and every Black person in the United States was an untouchable, that the land of the free had imposed a caste system similar to India's, and that he had lived under this system his entire life (Wilkerson 22).

The Bluest Eye explores caste and class. There is some mobility in the novel, though not for everyone. Pecola Breedlove goes mad, but Claudia MacTeer fights back and writes this novel, and while she is clearly depressed at the novel's end, she is not broken. Those who wish to ban *The Bluest Eye* object to introducing impressionable readers to what they consider obscene debasement of the Breedloves' lives, but they ignore that Toni Morrison also creates for readers useable alternatives in Claudia and other members of the MacTeer family.

Black bodies suffer because the world is unjust, in this novel and in in the real world. Authentic, caring love, like the love Mrs. MacTeer offers her daughters Frieda and Claudia, helps one face a sometimes-ruthless world. Trauma diminishes the lives of every character in this novel, but because of the way Toni Morrison creates her novel, because its narrator, Claudia MacTeer, questions and resists, one learns not to give up or give in, to face what one must face, a summer where Pecola's baby dies, where one sacrifices one's time and one's bicycle in order to try and save the life of Pecola's unborn child, but cannot. Pecola's blue eyes, her madness, breaks the reader's heart, but it also empowers the reader to both understand and fight for change, personal, cultural, and political. No one is "less than"; no one should be raped, not Cholly or Pecola. Readers can't hide from Soaphead Church and his brutality, or from Mr. Henry and his prurient insult, but readers can learn these characters' backstories, and readers can resist being a victim to twisted people's manipulations.

Toni Morrison wrote the book she needed to read when she created *The Bluest Eye* (Bigsby 251). Sunlight, clear observation, realistically and metaphorically, kill germs; censorship unequivocally causes blindness. Black girls need to learn from Pecola's madness and Claudia's resilience. Adults need to teach our children and ourselves to fight back against being treated unfairly, to survive and to take good care of ourselves so that we don't weather more than we must. Here's a good motto as we fight against racism, inequity, and weathering: "Fluctuat nec mergitor," "it is tossed by the wind but does not sink." This should be Claudia's mantra and it should be ours. We need to resist abuse of ourselves and others, to fight book bans, and by doing so allow readers convenient access to ideas that can help them understand their world and choose and make their place in it with less weathering. Humans need to heal their bodies and their hearts, and books like *The Bluest Eye* can help them to do so.

Ohio University

Works Cited and Consulted

Alter, Alexandra, Gilbert Cruz, and Elizabeth A. Harris. "A Fraught Chapter in American Education." *The New York Times*, 9 May 2023, p. A2.

Atlas, Marilyn. "The Issue of Literacy in America: Slave Narratives and Toni Morrison's *The Bluest Eye.*" *MidAmerica*, vol. 27, 2000, pp. 106–18.

Bennett, Juda, Winnifred Brown-Glaude, Cassandra Jackson, and Piper Kendrix Williams. "Why Black Folks Go Crazy." *The Toni Morrison Book Club*, U of Wisconsin P, pp. 38–62.

Bigsby, Christopher. "Jazz Queen." Interview with Toni Morrison. *The Independent* [London], 26 Apr. 1992, pp. 28–30.

De Waal, Frans. *The Bonobo and the Atheist: In Search of Humanism Among the Primates*. Norton, 2013.

Garcia, Raymond. "American Library Association Reports Record Number of Demands to Censor Library Books and Materials in 2022." *American Library Association*, 22 Mar. 2023, www.ala.org/news/press-releases/2023/03/record-book-bans-2022. Press release.

Geronimus, Arline T. *Weathering: The Extraordinary Stress of Ordinary Life in an Unjust Society*. Little, Brown Spark, 2023.

"Gov. Pritzker Signs Bill Making Illinois First State in the Nation to Outlaw Book Bans." *Illinois.gov*, 12 June 2023, www.illinois.gov/news/press-release.26575.html. Press release.

Gupta, Alisha Haridasani. "How 'Weathering' Contributes to Racial Health Disparities." *The New York Times*, 12 Apr. 2023, updated 14 Apr. 2023, www.nytimes.com/2023/04/12/well/live/weathering-health-racism-discrimination.html. Science Section.

Knox, Emily J. M. *Book Banning in the 21st-Century America*. Rowman and Littlefield, 2022.

Long, Lisa A. "A New Midwesternism in Toni Morrison's *The Bluest Eye.*" *Twentieth Century Literature*, vol. 59, no. 1, spring 2013, pp. 104–25.

Lorde, Audre. "The Master's Tools Will Never Dismantle the Master's House." *Sister Outsider: Essays and Speeches*. 1979. Crossing Press, 2007, pp. 110–13.

Morrison, Toni. *The Bluest Eye*. 1970. Vintage International, 2007.

———. Foreword. *The Bluest Eye*, pp. i–xiii.

———. "Invisible Ink: Reading the Writing and Writing the Reading." *Mouth Full of Blood: Essays, Speeches, Meditations*, Penguin, 2019, pp. 346–50.

Pastis, Stephan. "Pearls Before Swine." Cartoon. *Columbus Dispatch*, 11 Dec. 2023, p. 9B.

Smith, Mitch. "Judge Blocks Iowa's Ban on Certain Library Books." *The New York Times*, 31 Dec. 2023, p. 17.

Stegan, Anne. "Wentzville Schools to Allow *The Bluest Eye* in Libraries Again." *KSDK* [St. Louis], 25 Feb. 2022, www.ksdk.com/article/news/local/wentzville-schools-allow-bluest-eye-library-book-ban/63-8265d214-fb75-456f-9d5a-aa441f9e2b53.

"Top 13 Most Challenged Books of 2022." *American Library Association*, 21 Apr. 2023, www.ala.org/advocacy/bbooks/frequentlychallengedbooks/top10.

Wilkerson, Isabel. *Caste: The Origins of Our Discontents*. Random House, 2020.

Yip, Isabel, and Nicole Chavez. "Illinois Outlaws Book Bans in Public Libraries." *CNN*, 12 June 2023, updated 13 June 2023, www.cnn.com/2023/06/12/us/illinois-public-libraries-schools-book-bans/index.html.

WHO'S AFRAID OF BOOKS?

Banning Toni Morrison's *Beloved* in Michigan

Maureen N. Eke

Although book banning and challenging are not new, what is now new and alarming is the escalation of such actions, specifically targeting books by and about underrepresented groups. In their press release of November 29, 2021, the American Library Association states,

> In recent months, a few organizations have advanced the proposition that the voices of the marginalized have no place on library shelves. To this end, they have launched campaigns demanding the censorship of books and resources that mirror the lives of those who are gay, queer, or transgender or that tell the stories of persons who are Black, Indigenous, or persons of color. (Hlywak)

The American Library Association's press release underscores the repressive nature of these bans and challenges, pointing out the construction of false narratives to justify the silencing of authors from underrepresented groups. In this essay, I focus on the banning and/or challenging of Toni Morrison's Pulitzer Prize–winning novel *Beloved* (1987) in Michigan. Morrison's novel is a reworking of the story of the historical Margaret Garner, a Kentucky slave woman who escaped into Ohio in 1856 with her family. But when slave catchers, under the 1850s Slave Act, came to return her to Kentucky, she cut the throat of her young child to protect her from slavery. During Garner's trial, the question was whether to charge her with murder or destruction of property. The novel begins in the 1870s, years after the end of slavery and explores the antebellum period and the period immediately after it. Morrison has indicated that in writing this novel she did not attempt to conduct additional research about the fate of Margaret Garner beyond the article about her that Morrison found.

For the purposes of this essay, I will adopt PEN America's definition of book ban/challenge. According to PEN America,

> A school book ban [is] any action taken against a book based on its content and as a result of parent or community challenges, administrative decisions, or in response to direct or threatened action by lawmakers or other governmental officials, that leads to a previously accessible book being either completely removed from availability to students, or where access to a book is restricted or diminished. ("Book Bans")

There are only a few instances of book ban/challenge for Toni Morrison's *Beloved* in Michigan. These include one instance in Plymouth-Canton Community Schools in 2012 and the other in Gladwin Community Schools in May 2022. Plymouth-Canton is a semi-urban setting located near Detroit, Michigan. Gladwin is a rural community in central Michigan. While the Plymouth-Canton book challenge/ban was resolved—the school district voted to keep *Beloved*—"PEN America Index of School Book Bans—2021–2022" indicates that Gladwin Community Schools has "banned [*Beloved*] pending investigation." In these two cases, two different entities initiated the ban or challenge. In Plymouth-Canton, two parents called for the ban, whereas in Gladwin Community Schools, PEN America identifies the "origin of challenge" as an "administrator." Upon further investigation, I was informed that the Gladwin Community Schools party engaged in the review of the book did not complete its task. Consequently, *Beloved* was not removed or banned from the school library.[1] Although these bans/challenges are only a few instances, they are worth noting, because these bans/challenges make a mockery of Michigan's history of anti-slavery activity. The State of Michigan played an important role in the anti-slavery movement with various cities, including Ann Arbor, Adrian, and Detroit serving as important stops or stations on the Michigan Underground Railroad. Michigan's anti-slavery movement began in the early 1830s. In fact, Michigan's Constitution of 1835, Article XI prohibits slavery and reads, "Neither slavery nor involuntary servitude shall ever be introduced into this state, except for the punishment of crimes of which the party shall have been duly convicted" (Michigan State, "Constitution 1835"). This article sits alone. But in 1850, the prohibition of slavery would become Section 11 under Article 18 with modified language (Michigan State, "Constitution 1850"). Today, the Michigan Constitution still bans slavery in Article 1, section 9. The language reads, "Neither slavery, nor involuntary servitude unless for the punishment of crime, shall ever be tolerated in this state" (Michigan State, "Constitution 1963"). If Morrison's proto-slave narrative is inspired by the story of the historical Margaret Garner's resistance to slavery (an act supported by Michigan's constitution), one would expect contemporary Michiganders to recognize, protect, or honor that history. Banning the book does not seem to do so. So, what about the novel compels those who wish to silence it?

Beloved explores important and complex eras of American history, specifically, the antebellum period and the period immediately after it. The novel also asks its audience to look deeply, to reconcile with a past, even if that past is as frightening as that revealed in the book. But banning or challenging *Beloved* rejects that reconciliation; indeed, it refuses the possibility of any healing or recuperation of the past. The American Library Association article cited above adds,

> Falsely claiming that these [banned and/or challenged] works are subversive, immoral, or worse, these groups induce elected and non-elected officials to abandon constitutional principles, ignore the rule of law, and disregard individual rights to promote government censorship of library collections. Some of these groups even resort to intimidation and threats to achieve their ends, targeting the safety and livelihoods of library workers, educators, and board members who have dedicated themselves to public service, informing our communities, and educating our youth. (Hlywak)

There is extensive evidence of the various ways in which the erasure of knowledge, history, and rights have been enforced, particularly against authors, texts, and cultures perceived as "threatening" to whatever has been constructed as an American way of life—the American dream or an imagined perfect America—a single story.

"Create a single story, show a people as one thing, as only one thing, over and over again, and that is what they become," Chimamanda Ngozi Adichie says in her TED Talk, "The Danger of a Single Story." Adichie's comment is relevant here, because an implication of the book challenges or bans is the postulation that any other version of America's story that does not align with what the challengers define as the "true narrative" is wrong, that is, antithetical to a "true" American story. As such, those calling for banning *Beloved* argue that the book does not represent them or "real" American history; others claim that it contains language portraying gratuitous violence and sexual acts.

The desire to protect America from those who want to denigrate it would become clear to me in late 2021 while attending several school board meetings in a semi-rural community when some parents were protesting the teaching of Critical Race Theory (CRT). They wanted the school curriculum purged of any content that suggested "CRT." After several comments by these parents, I realized that at the core of the censorship was a desire to define American-ness, specifically patriotism. Several "CRT"-protesting parents asserted various times that those who supported the teaching of "CRT" were making their children feel guilty and making "us," meaning "Americans," look bad, never mind that no one in K-12 schools is teaching Critical Race Theory or any race theory. These parents did not want the discussion of The 1619 Project either because of its strident linking of American identity to slavery and racism ("The 1619 Project"). These parents did not want the inclusion of slavery in the school curriculum. I countered, explaining that slavery is an important part of American history and should be part of the curriculum. But for these parents, it is unpatriotic to teach works that "made" them or their children "feel guilty" about being American. My attempt to engage, connect with a parent who wanted to "talk" at the end of the meeting was futile. I offered a quick catalog—several books, including Maya Angelou's *I Know Why the Caged Bird Sings* (1969); Frederick Douglass's *Narrative of the Life of Frederick Douglass* (1845); Toni Morrison's *The Bluest Eye* (1970) and *Beloved* (1977); and Alice Walker's *The Color Purple* (1982)—but this parent was uninterested in stories that would make him feel bad or represented America negatively. He wanted "real history."

Beloved, another parent declared to me, did not represent "real history." It is "horrible," she said when she accosted me outside the school building. "Why would anyone read it?" When I asked if she had read it, she said "no, but I heard that there is sex, rape, and infanticide. It is not history!" A parallel objection is to The 1619 Project, which many of the anti-"woke" and anti-CRT parents want to ban. It is un-American, all "lies," the same group of people proclaimed again and again over several meetings. A parent confessed that she had not read the book but had been told it was "horrible" and did not need to read it to insist that it should be banned. One cannot help but continue to ask, how is it horrible? Why the objection? "What history should we not teach or talk about?" "What exactly are you afraid of?" I asked once.

In some part, the protesting parents' comments about the narrative are correct. The subject matter is "horrible." Slavery is horrible! But it is not the horror of slavery that the parents seem to object to so much as the realization that the horror is an American horror, and it is theirs! It's a traumatic gothic past that haunts the nation and ultimately haunts the consciousness of those who look closely at it. But the refusal to confront the horror is couched in other language, primarily focused on the text's representation of sexuality, sexual violence, and/or nudity, what some have referred to as "gratuitous sex" or pornography. Here also lies the challenge to exploring slavery. How does one discuss slavery without looking at the accompanying violence—sexual or not? How can we engage in a critical exploration of slavery that does not uncover the sexual violence, the rape of the Black female slave, and various violations of the Black body?

A simple search on Google for information on the banning or challenging of Toni Morrison's *Beloved* reveals that it is one of two of Morrison's texts frequently targeted for banning or challenging. The other is *The Bluest Eye*. PEN America's "Index of School Book Bans—2021–2022" indicates eleven instances of banning/challenging for *Beloved* during this school year and ten instances in the 2022–23 school year. Most of these instances are in Florida, a response to Governor Ron DeSantis's anti-CRT stance and book bans, which he now calls a "'hoax' from news outlets." According to WLRN Miami/South Florida, "Gov. Ron DeSantis pushed back on what he says is a 'hoax' from news outlets claiming the state is banning mass amounts of books from school libraries and classrooms" (Lebron). Commenting on the case of Florida, Olivia B. Waxman writes that "in Florida's Polk County Morrison's *The Bluest Eye* and *Beloved* were among 16 books 'quarantined'—taken off shelves in public school libraries so 'thorough, thoughtful review of the content can take place.'" But other states have joined Florida and engaged in similar acts of erasure or attempts to silence history and Morrison. There are also earlier instances before 2021. Marshall University library tracks the banning and challenging of Morrison's *Beloved* to 2007, when the book was challenged but "[r]etained on the Northwest Suburban HS District 214 reading list in Arlington Heights (IL) along with eight other challenged titles." However, it was "[p]ulled from the senior AP English class at Eastern HS in Louisville (KY) because two parents complained that the Pulitzer Prize–winning novel about antebellum slavery depicted the inappropriate topics of bestiality, racism and sex" ("Banned Books 2022"). The library website continues, noting that in 2016, the book was challenged on the Fairfax County (VA) senior English reading list by a parent, who claimed "the book includes scenes of violent sex, including a gang rape, and was too graphic and extreme for teenagers." The university library webpage adds, "The controversy led to legislation (House Bill S16) that calls for the Virginia Department of Education to create a policy that notifies parents of the content and then allows them to review the materials" ("Banned Books 2022").

But in Michigan, earlier instances point to the Plymouth-Canton Community Schools, in 2011–13, where Anna Clark says, "two parents who thought the novel was inappropriate tried to ban the book." The Marshall University Library website identifies the two cases (2012 and 2013) as originating in Salem High School, one of the Plymouth-Canton Community High Schools where the book was "challenged, but retained as a text in … Advanced Placement English courses." In both cases, the "complainants cited the allegedly obscene nature of some passages in the book and asked that it be removed from the curriculum" ("Banned Books 2022").

According to Leah Drayton of the New York Public Library, "Through all her renown, Morrison's books are a regular fixture on the American Library Association

(ALA)'s Frequently Challenged Books list, with her novels *Beloved* and *The Bluest Eye* consistently challenged in schools and libraries." Morrison's novels, which explore the Black experiences from slavery through Reconstruction to World War I and the Jim Crow era, have been challenged for their dogged exposition of racism, violence, sexism, and the resulting trauma.

Trauma, Margaret Garner, and History

The central argument of *Beloved* is that slavery was traumatic, so traumatizing that a woman would be compelled to kill her helpless baby as an act of love to protect her from a life in slavery. By that action Sethe, the character modeled after Margaret Garner, asserts her right as a human being with dignity and reclaims her autonomy as a mother, the owner of the body that "birthed" the dead child. These are rights that slavery does not accord her, because slavery defines her and her child only as property. In her poem "The Slave Mother," Frances E. W. Harper dramatizes the anguish and helplessness of a slave mother who cannot save her child who is being separated from her. As Harper laments, "He is not hers, although she bore / For him a mother's pains; / He is not hers, although her blood / Is coursing through his veins!" (lines 17–20). Sethe is cognizant of the inhumanity of slave laws that declare her as property and under which she cannot claim ownership of her children. Hence, to escape slavery, she sent them ahead to Ohio with her mother-in-law Baby Suggs to protect them from Sweet Home. Besides, the Fugitive Slave Act of 1850 empowered local sheriffs, slave catchers, or any white person (who could be deputized) to capture and return to slavery fugitive Blacks, even if they were caught in free states. Freed Blacks were also victimized by this law. The case of Solomon Northrup, who, although free-born, was abducted and sold into slavery, is worth mentioning. He spent twelve years as a slave before becoming free. Like Northrup, Sethe had no protection under the law. So, when Sethe saw "the four horsemen" who had come to retrieve her and her children from freedom in Ohio and return them to slavery in Kentucky, she did the only thing she could—resist, save her children, "carried, pushed, dragged them," placing them "[o]ver there. Outside this place, where they would be safe" (163). With this single act, Sethe declares her autonomy.

It is not only Sethe who claims power, but also Morrison who asserts the right to determine how the story of Black experiences in the United States is rendered. In this narrative, Morrison dares to engage in a critique of American history, writ large, exposing its horrors, violence, and challenging her readers to contend with a nightmarish past. In so doing, the author engages in the work of "rememory" as Sethe and Morrison refer to the act of psychic recuperation of a "disremembered" past.

Sadly, in calling for the removal of Morrison's book because it represents sexual violence perceived as too "graphic and extreme for teenagers," the proponents engage in the erasure of history, but especially the silencing of Morrison. Indeed, it is the equivalent of killing the messenger because one does not like the message. Those who object to the novel's content seem to miss the narrative's argument that slavery violated individual human rights and dignity by dehumanizing those enslaved. Sethe acts to restore those rights. Otherwise, how does one explain a mother's killing of her child as an act of love? How does the narrative help us to engage with topics related to social justice such as human rights, civil rights, and the preservation of human dignity? For those preoccupied with morality and Christian ethics, the narrative provides an opportunity to examine Christian charity—love thy neighbor as thyself or do unto others as thou wish them to do unto thee—the very ethic which slave-holding Christians violated. Indeed, Frederick Douglass calls attention to this contradiction in slave-holding Christians in his autobiography, *Narrative of the Life of Frederick Douglass*, where he draws a distinction between what he describes as "the pure, peaceable, and impartial Christianity of Christ" and "the corrupt, slaveholding, women-whipping, cradle-plundering, partial and hypocritical Christianity of this land" (389). Sethe's choice and action suggest that she is very aware of the "horrible inconsistencies" in the practice of Christian and American justice among slave-holding Christians. No law protected her and her children from slavery. Moreover, as Douglass adds, the Christian slaveholder, "the warm defender of the sacredness of the family relation is the same that scatters whole families,--sundering husbands and wives, parents and children, sisters and brothers …" (389). For Sethe, these are her realities as a slave woman, and they would be her children's. She was separated from her mother as a child; she was separated often from her husband Halle; then, she was separated from her children when they travelled to Ohio without her. Also, Sethe knows that Baby Suggs, her mother-in-law, had been separated from most of her children, who were sold away from her. For Sethe, Schoolteacher and the sheriff's arrival in her home in Ohio where she had lived freely with her family for many months signaled the death of her freedom.

Morrison has indicated in interviews and essays that her novel is not a documentary of slavery, but an attempt to provide her readers with a "narrow and deep" representation of slavery rather than an epic sweep. She had found an article about the historical Margaret Garner, "the slave woman who killed her child." She did not want to know the details of the historical Margaret Garner's life but wanted to rely on her imagination ("Rediscovering Black History"). For instance, in the novel, Morrison does not focus on the trial. While Margaret Garner's story is individual and personal, it is also collective and national. As stated elsewhere, "[The] novel serves as a vehicle for examining slavery as a traumatizing historical event at various levels: individual, group, and national" (Eke 3). The narrative challenges its audience to revisit an unspeakable past and, perhaps, to reconcile with it. But such past as Sethe observes may not be reconcilable and for some may be a story not to tell or simply left "out there in the world" (Morrison, *Beloved* 43). Banning the book will not resolve the horror nor will it stop the haunting of America's consciousness. The call to ban it seems to be located at an ambiguous space, where the history of slavery with its horrors confronts the growing national refusal to acknowledge that racism and the legacy of slavery persist in the nation. The arguments presented for banning the novel and removing it from libraries or school curriculum vary: some focus on the graphic violence in the novel; others complain about Morrison's description of sexual violence experienced by Black women under slavery, calling it pornographic; other challengers claim that it is inappropriate for students because of its content and language as in the case of Plymouth-Canton Community Schools in Michigan. Barb Dame, one of the two complaining parents, argued "that Beloved was a fictitious account set upon its real-life backdrop of slavery, and contained gratuituous [sic] language, violence and sex acts that provide no historical context for the reader" (McKay). For sure, these parents are correct in pointing out the graphic violence—sexual or otherwise. But the narrative contextualizes these acts as representative of the dehumanizing nature of slavery. How does one render the horrors of slavery visually without it being "graphic"? Is there a way to romanticize the traumatizing and horrific nature of slavery?

Anna Clark, of Michigan Radio (NPR), notes that "at a two-hour public review … [the two parents] complained that the novels [*Beloved* and one other book] contain passages that discuss sex, ghosts and the killing of an infant. Mr. Dame [one of the parents] also said that characters in the books take God's name in vain." According to the article, "[at] a public hearing, one parent argued that *Beloved* was given a Lexile rating that equates to a 5th-grade reading level," a measure used to determine a "text's usefulness for teaching people to read" (Clark). Clark continues,

> The protesting parents weren't really bothered by Lexile's measure of *Beloved*, either. The real reason behind their challenge was that the novel was deemed an inappropriately "fictitious" account about the real-life issue of slavery. With this backdrop in mind, they argued that the language, violence and sex acts provide no historical context for the reader—never mind that language, violence and sex acts are far from out of context in slavery.

As Clark points out, for the parents, the Lexile measure seems less urgent than how historically real the narrative is. Indeed, the parents impose a moral ethic on the novel because it is a fictionalized rendering of history, thus claiming that it is "bad." Moreover, as Mr. Dame said, "it takes God's name in vain," forget that slave holders were engaged in similar acts of taking "God's name in vain." Missing is any serious critical engagement with the novel's artistic and literary qualities or the value of the novel as a work of fiction that engages history. Consequently, the parents failed to notice the literary aesthetics and complex poetic use of language in Morrison's novel. Also, one cannot miss the absurdity of comparing the reading level of Morrison's Pulitzer Award–winning novel to that of a children's novel! Brian Read, the AP English teacher, however, defended his choice of *Beloved*, saying "AP English Literature, it's about fiction," … "Poetry and fiction" (McKay). Besides, he has "taught Beloved for 10 years, never had it challenged." While acknowledging the parents' desire to protect their children, the teacher added that the novel has literary significance: "the themes in Beloved, which tells the story of the ghost of a deceased child apparently coming back to visit her mother, feature 'magical realism,' where the very fantastical can be mundane, and the book has several instances of symbolism" (McKay).

Furthermore, if there are violence and sex acts in the novel, it is because they are representative of the experiences of Black women under slavery. In his autobiography, another frequently banned book, Douglass describes instances of Black women who were bred by the slave plantation owners who wanted to improve their wealth. His aunt Hester was beaten by her angry master until her back bled. Similarly, Sethe shows Paul D the scars left on her back by the beating she received from Schoolteacher and his boys after she revealed that they "took [her] milk" (16). Certainly, these violent acts speak to Black women's experiences under slavery. To claim that they are gratuitous pornography and justification for banning the novel is a red herring. What seems objectionable is the book's reconstruction of and engagement with a past that cannot easily be glorified or "airbrushed" and romanticized. It is gory, unpleasant, unthinkable, and it is a past where Mrs. Garner's "Sweet Home" plantation is no longer sweet or home. For Sethe, "Sweet Home" represents the site of physical and psychic wounding that haunts her as equally as the ghost of her dead child. At Sweet Home, Schoolteacher's violence reigned. Sweet Home was the place of destruction of lives, where Schoolteacher "broke three more Sweet Home [Black] men, and punched the glittering iron out of Sethe's eyes, leaving two open wells that did not reflect firelight" (9). Morrison's language underscores the violence of slavery. How could the complaining parents not hear Morrison's witnessing even in these early passages? Where is their empathy? How could these parents not honor Sethe's mourning of her body and humanity when she describes to Paul D the atrocity visited upon her after his escape from Sweet Home? She tells Paul D, "After I left you, those boys came in there and took my milk. That's what they came in there for. He held me down and took it" (16). Her baby's breast milk was stolen by white men, who not only dehumanized her, but also denied her baby nourishment. Sethe, however, was determined to claim both her bodily autonomy and her dignity and in so doing, restore her humanity when she reported her horrible experience to Mrs. Garner, a white woman! Clearly, Mrs. Garner understood and recognized the harm Sethe had experienced, because even though she "couldn't speak … her eyes rolled out tears" (16–17). She showed sympathy for an enslaved Black woman! But when the boys found out, they whipped Sethe with cowhide that left a sprawling "chokecherry" tree on her back, a graphic reminder of their power and her trauma. Morrison's book seeks to capture Sethe's anguish, the cry of a mother, agonized that her baby might suffer or die either from the starvation of not having her nourishment or from the horrors of being enslaved. "They took my milk," she repeated to Paul D.

Reactions—Black History:
"It's not going to be all flowers and daisies; it's going to be ugly."

Interestingly, the students affected by Plymouth-Canton School District's book banning/challenge recognize the importance of Morrison's text. In her interview with some of these students, Jennifer Guerra notes that several of the students were displeased with the decision to ban or remove the book. "Meredith Yancy, 16, is reading the book in her Advanced Placement English Literature class at Salem High School. She says she didn't have a problem with the book's mature content" (Guerra). Salem High is in Plymouth-Canton School District. Yancy clearly understands that slavery was horrible, when she states, "I handled it just fine. Slavery, that's a really serious issue. And a lot of events in the book are not there to be gratuitous and offensive; they're there to make a point of how awful those times really were" (Guerra). Despite the objections of the two parents (adults) who called for the banning of Beloved, the 16-year-old Yancy (not yet an adult) underscores the gravity of the topic, shows appreciation for the history and past that Morrison's narrative reveals. Events are there "to make a point," as is Morrison. Guerra adds that another 16-year-old student, Alexis Bentley, stated that she was 'offended' when she heard of the possible banning of Beloved. According to Guerra, Bentley, who is African American, said, "African-American history is not pretty.... It's not going to be all flowers and daisies; it's going to be ugly, and there are going to be times where you're going to be appalled at what's in the history. But it's education" (Guerra).

In her essay "Rediscovering Black History," Morrison underscores that "for larger and larger numbers of black people [a] sense of loss has grown and the deeper the conviction that something valuable is slipping away from us, the more necessary it has become to find some way to hold on to the useful past without blocking off the possibilities of the future. To create something that might last, that would bear witness to the quality and variety of black life …" (42). Her curated work, *The Black Book* (Harris), a collection of extant materials, including articles, photographs, slave auction posters, songs, and images of Blacks and the Black experience from the seventeenth century to the twentieth up to 1974, bears such witness. The book contains a reproduction of an 1856 article from *The American Baptist* under the title, "A Visit to the Slave Mother Who Killed Her Child" (Harris 10), which serves as the source for Morrison's *Beloved*. So, like *The Black Book, Beloved* represents Morrison's attempt "to create something that might last" … that "would bear witness to the quality and variety of black life," as Morrison states above. "Whatever that something was, it would have to be honest, would have to be rendered through our own collective consciousness," she adds ("Rediscovering" 42). In short, Morrison's comments ask us to contemplate who tells the story of slavery and of Margaret Garner. And how it is told.

Indeed, one must applaud the two students for underscoring the educational value of *Beloved* and its attempt to represent a painful past. It is truth that must be told. And, as Morrison writes, "unmonitored writing" is trouble. "Truth is trouble," she adds. "It is trouble for the warmonger, the torturer, the corporate thief, the political hack, the corrupt justice system, and for a comatose public. Unpersecuted, unjailed, unharassed writers are trouble for the ignorant bully, the sly racist, and the predators feeding off the world's resources" ("Peril" 2). Morrison was prescient, anticipatory of the current trend to ban or challenge books perceived as threatening. Her essay "Peril" from which the passages above are taken was copyrighted in 2009, and how apropos it is to the current situation, where politicians now have become book critics, seizing any opportunity to use their objection to books as a trojan horse to silence narratives about groups who have been marginalized.

In 2021, Virginia Republican gubernatorial candidate Glenn Youngkin used his conservative platform to wage war against Critical Race Theory (CRT). Deploying his anti-CRT rhetoric, he whipped up fear among MAGA and conservative parents, promising to give them more voice in the education of their children by banning books the parents claimed were objectionable. Then, he recruited Laura Murphy—a parent—who had called for banning *Beloved* in 2013, claiming that it gave her son nightmares, as his ally and the face of Youngkin's promise to parents. Then, they both targeted Toni Morrison's *Beloved* as their exemplum for their book banning project (Blest). One cannot help but note the irony in these cases. Toni Morrison's narrative about the quest for freedom in an American midwestern non-slave holding state (Ohio) is seen as threatening and historically unimportant.

In the Plymouth-Canton Schools' case, the parents' complaint about *Beloved* is absurd. Truly, no discussion of slavery will be complete without a critical examination of Black women's experiences under that horrible institution. Is it possible to engage in a just and honest conversation of American slavery without acknowledging that Black women were raped, bred, sold, murdered, and separated from their families? Slavery was horrible, a fact that the two 16-year-old students I mentioned earlier underscore, but the students also acknowledge that the story of slavery is part of the larger American narrative. They reject the removal of the book from their curriculum because it constitutes the silencing of certain voices. In their press release on January 20, 2012, the ACLU of Michigan sided with the students and parents who were protesting the ban. The ACLU stated that in their letter of the same date to the Plymouth-Canton School District, they asked the school district to "respect the constitutional rights of students and not ban the award-winning novels *Beloved* and *Waterland* from the Advanced Placement English curriculum" (ACLU of Michigan). The press release also notes that the organization reminded the school district that "the US Supreme Court has held repeatedly that banning books because they offend some runs afoul of the First Amendment." Unlike Youngkin's "comatose" parents, the parents at Plymouth-Canton Schools were awake or "woke" to appropriate the verbiage today. They were outraged and they protested, flooding the school board meeting, "flowing out into the halls. All but Matt and Barb Dame—the two protesting parents—spoke against banning the books" (Lessenberry). Although Youngkin would succeed in banning *Beloved* in Virginia, the Plymouth-Canton, Michigan, school board voted to keep the book in the AP English curriculum.

Claiming pornography in the case of Morrison's *Beloved* is a red herring. The narrative represents sexual violence as a traumatic characteristic of slavery that dehumanized and bestialized Black bodies, especially Black women as discussed earlier. Besides, according to PEN America's "The Freedom to Write," "Librarians and educators choose books for their literary and educational value. Books banned in American schools do not fit the well-established legal and colloquial definitions of 'pornography' or 'indecency'" ("Book Bans"). Unlike the two students mentioned earlier, what seems objectionable to these parents is how to explain the racism or racial violence present in the banned or challenged books as an American legacy. How does one reconcile the story of slavery and the denial of rights with an "imagined" image of America that promises its people "justice," "domestic tranquility," and "a more perfect Union" where "all men are created equal … with certain unalienable rights … among these … life, liberty and the pursuit of Happiness?" In short, how does one explain the incomprehensible, the horror, the traumatizing brutality and inhumanity, the denial of those "unalienable rights" and the promised privileges to certain groups, including women?

Currently, any discussion of racial oppression or racism is seen as teaching Critical Race Theory (CRT), the catch-all term or monster for all conversations about racism. Morrison's *Beloved*, for instance, is one of the books that these parents charge with teaching Critical Race Theory or CRT. Indeed, the focus of these groups is to expose schools teaching CRT; as such, the book bans serve as a conduit for eliminating any book they believe is engaged in discussions of racial oppression or racism. According to Emily Knox, the book bannings, "are tied to whatever is causing anxiety in society" (qtd. in Waxman). In the case of *Beloved*, CRT has been conflated with discussions of slavery, racism, and its history. The subject of *Beloved* is discomforting. There is no mercy for Sethe or the historical Margaret Garner and Morrison does not spare her reader from witnessing the atrocities. *Beloved*'s content is too unbearable. In her essay "Reckoning with Beloved," Amy Frykholm writes,

> When a Virginia parent complained recently that her son, a high school senior, experienced "night terrors" after reading *Beloved*, I wanted to congratulate the woman on having raised such a profoundly sensitive son. Here was a person who could feel the horrors of that book in his own body and soul. What a gift. If he could feel that, then maybe there is hope for all of us, as we try to reckon with American history, with slavery and the world it bequeathed to us. (12)

In this historical novel, Morrison bears witness to history, reinscribing it through the lenses of the group most affected by it. Yes, it is Sethe's (historical Margaret Garner's) individual story, but it is also the collective story of Blacks in America, and it is a national, writ American story. Sethe emerges out of the narrative as a reconfiguration of a "dismembered" and "unaccounted for" Margaret Garner whom Morrison excavated from an old newspaper article. Ironically like the parents who want to protect their children from the nightmare of history, Sethe is a Black mother also fighting to protect her child from the same nightmare, and indeed, to preserve her own humanity as a mother. It is about motherhood or mothering. The work asks us to consider what a mother would do to save her child, the "fruit" or "product" of her body? I cannot help but recall the biblical story of King Solomon's decision, when faced with two mothers who came to him claiming the same child. Solomon declared that he would sever the child in two and give each half. The true mother cried out to Solomon to spare the child and offer it to the other woman. Margaret Garner, or Sethe in the novel, may not be King Solomon, but her decision is as dramatic—she loved her child so much that she sacrificed her, letting her go to save her from being dirtied, "so bad you couldn't like yourself anymore" (*Beloved* 251). As Denver narrates in the novel, slavery dirtied the individual and Sethe resisted it through her children. Denver observes,

The best thing she was, was her children. Whites might dirty her all right, but not *her* best thing, her beautiful, magical best thing—the part of her that was clean. No undreamable dreams about whether the headless, feetless torso hanging in the tree with a sign on it was her husband or Paul A; whether the bubbling-hot girls in the colored-school fire set by patriots included her daughter; whether a gang of whites invaded her daughter's private parts, soiled her daughter's thighs and threw her daughter out of the wagon. She might have to work the slaughterhouse yard, but not her daughter.

And no one, nobody on this earth, would list her daughter's characteristics on the animal side of the paper. No. Oh no. (251)

For sure, Morrison's language shocks the reader: it is graphic, gory, heart wrenching, and haunting. But so was slavery. With its first sentence—"124 was spiteful" (3)—the novel propels its reader into Sethe's story without warning and Morrison is unapologetic. Commenting on the opening declarative sentence of the novel, "124 was spiteful," she says, "Whatever the risks of confronting the reader with what must be immediately incomprehensible in that simple, declarative authoritative sentence, the risk of unsettling him or her, I determined to take" ("Black Matter(s)" 195). In taking this risk, Morrison claims agency as a Black griotte, raconteur, storyteller, oral historian. Black people, as do other people, want to tell their own stories and to tell it differently. *Beloved* accomplishes this task. It is "[f]ull of a baby's venom" (3). It is a different story of American history and specifically of Black experience. It may not be coherent with the myth of the American dream, of a beautiful American history, but it is Black America's story—uniquely theirs! Banning this book, removing it from public space, denies Blacks the right to speak their own truth. As Adichie contends, stories are important. However, a single story is dangerous; it is destructive. "How they are told, who tells them, when they're told, how many stories are told, are really dependent on power" (Adichie). Morrison's *Beloved* undermines that single story of America and especially of Blacks in America as told by white America.

African American Spirituality: Healing the Community

Although the novel's organizing event is Sethe's killing of her daughter, Morrison presents us with other aspects of Black life. We meet Baby Suggs, Sethe's mother-in-law and woodland healer/preacher/prophet who helps the community restore itself. Through Baby Suggs, Morrison provides readers with a glimpse African American spirituality. Baby Suggs is ancestor and healer/preacher. In a clearing in the woods, Baby Suggs leads her people through self-recovery. Slowly, guiding them to claim themselves, returning to them their bodies, parts of themselves that slavery has "dirtied," dismembered, forgotten, and commodified, she calls them forward:

> Here … in this here place, we flesh; flesh that weeps, laughs; flesh that dances on bare feet in grass. Love it. Love it hard. Yonder they do not love your flesh. They despise it. They don't love your eyes. They'd just as soon pick em out. No more do they love the skin on your back. Yonder they flay it. And O my people they do not love your hands. Those they only use, tie, bind, chop off and leave empty. Love your hands! Love them. Raise them up and kiss them. Touch others with them, pat them together, stroke them on your face 'cause they don't love that either. You got to love it, you! (88)

Even though Baby Suggs catalogs the atrocities her people have experienced, this is a moment of self-recuperation. She grants them permission to reclaim their bodies and their spirits. Baby Suggs's language is poetic, empathetic, and healing. Likewise, at the end of the novel, Sethe is healed too, when the Black community organizes itself and exorcizes the ghost of Beloved. By so doing, they save Sethe from Beloved's destructive wrath, and they also save themselves. Morrison signals the possibility of healing when Sethe accepts herself. Paul D tells her, "You your best thing, Sethe. You are," to which she responds, "Me? Me?" (273). For sure, she is questioning Paul D's claim, but there is awareness of the possibility of hope. But by focusing primarily on the novel's representation of the violence of slavery, including the sexual violence, those who want to ban the novel miss other important aspects of the book, including Morrison's artistry.

Closing

In her TED Talk, "The Danger of a Single Story," Chimamanda Ngozi Adichie reminds us of the relationship between a "single story" and access to power. "Create a single story, show a people as one thing, as only one thing, over and over again, and that is what they become." Those who have access to power weave a single story of the disempowered. The legacies of slavery and racism have disempowered and continue to marginalize Blacks in America. Those who want to ban *Beloved* have a single story of what America is or ought to be. It is not inclusive. It maintains the legacies of slavery and racism and does not recognize the story that Toni Morrison and authors who assert difference wish to tell. But as Morrison has noted, writers have a responsibility to tell the "truth" even about the traumas visited upon us. She asserts, "Certain kinds of trauma visited on people are so deep, so cruel, that unlike money, unlike vengeance, even unlike justice, or rights, or the good-will of others, only writers can translate such trauma and turn sorrow into meaning, sharpening the moral imagination" ("Peril" 4). Indeed, Morrison's assertion suggests that writers have a responsibility to society—to help recuperate horrible pasts or experiences—to help society heal. She writes because it is imperative "to save ourselves" (5).

As narrative, *Beloved* helps us to "rememory," remember, "piece together" our unresolved past. Similarly, the character Beloved, the ghost who walks in and out of the narrative, embodies our past, bringing it into the present to confront us and Sethe, reminding us of a story that we "refuse to remember" or tell. Perhaps, "remembering [seems] unwise," to echo Morrison in the closing pages of her novel. Perhaps, the story of slavery and its atrocities is "not a story to pass on" (274). But perhaps, it is "a story" that we must "pass on," to dislodge the traumatic horrors of a history that we have "disremembered" and that remains not fully "accounted for." It is the task of the writer to engage the public with such important revelations and conversations about society. As John Updike puts it, "We must write where we stand; wherever we do stand, there is life; and an imitation of life we know, however narrow, is our only ground" (10). Morrison's *Beloved* is an imitation of Margaret Garner's story and a representation of the story of slavery, an American reality too! As such, the call to purge the story of the atrocities or the painful aspect of that history seems to be a call to represent falsehood. This is peril. It would contradict Updike's assertion, because "[a]t the center of Morrison's creative life are the experiences of African Americans from slavery to the present" (Eke 22). Banning *Beloved* either in Michigan or elsewhere undermines Morrison's fierce commitment to recuperate African American history and heritage and in so doing to help to complete the story of America.

Central Michigan University

Note

1. I called Gladwin Community Schools twice seeking some update about the banning. I was told that *Beloved* is still available in the school library because the party that was charged with reviewing the banning did not complete the review.

Works Cited

Adichie, Chimamanda Ngozi. "The Danger of a Single Story." *YouTube*, uploaded by TED, 7 Oct. 2009, www.youtube.com/watch?v=D9Ihs241zeg. Accessed 14 Oct. 2023.

American Civil Liberties Union (ACLU) of Michigan. "Books Must Not Be Banned, ACLU Tells Plymouth-Canton Schools." *ACLU*, 20 Jan. 2012, www.aclu.org/press-releases/books-must-not-be-banned-aclu-tells-plymouth-canton-schools. Press release. Accessed 14 Oct. 2023.

"Banned Books 2022—*Beloved*." Marshall Libraries, www.marshall.edu/library/bannedbooks/beloved/. Accessed 19 Sept. 2023.

Blest, Paul. "Mom Who Tried to Ban Toni Morrison's 'Beloved' Is Now a GOP Star." *Vice News*, 26 Oct. 2021, www.vice.com/en/article/mom-who-tried-to-ban-toni-morrison-beloved-glenn-youngkin/. Accessed 14 Oct. 2023.

"Book Bans: Frequently Asked Questions." *PEN America*, pen.org/book-bans-frequently-asked-questions/.

Clark, Anna. "How Toni Morrison's 'Beloved' Is Taught in Schools," *The Daily Beast*, 4 Oct. 2012, updated 14 July 2017, www.thedailybeast.com/how-toni-morrisons-beloved-is-taught-in-schools. Accessed 14 Oct. 2023.

Douglass, Frederick. "Narrative of the Life of Frederick Douglass." *The Norton Anthology of African American Literature*, edited by Henry Louis Gates and Valerie Smith, 3rd ed., vol. 1, W. W. Norton & Company, 2014, pp. 326–91.

Drayton, Leah. "Truth Is Trouble: Toni Morrison's Advocacy Against Censorship." *New York Public Library*, September 14, 2022, www.nypl. org/blog/2022/09/14/truth-trouble-toni-morrisons-advocacy-against-censorship. Accessed 19 Sept. 2023. Blog.

Eke, Maureen N. "Mapping Toni Morrison's *Beloved:* Of Love, History, Trauma, and Healing." *Critical Insights: Beloved*, edited by Maureen N. Eke, Salem Press/Grey House Publishing, 2015.

Frykholm, Amy. "Reckoning with *Beloved.*" *The Christian Century*, vol. 139, no. 10, 18 May 2022, pp. 12–13. *ProQuest*.

Guerra, Jennifer. "A Michigan School District Considers Banning Two Books." *Michigan Public NPR*, 17 Jan. 2012, www.michiganradio.org/education/2012-01-17/a-michigan-school-district-considers-banning-two-books. Accessed 19 Sept. 2023.

Harper, Frances Ellen Watkins. "The Slave Mother." *Poetry Foundation*, www. poetryfoundation.org/poems/51977/the-slave-mother-56d23017ceaad. Accessed 1 Nov. 2023.

Harris, A. Middleton, et al. *The Black Book.* 1974. Random House, 2009.

Hlywak, Stephanie. "The American Library Association Opposes Widespread Efforts to Censor Books in U.S. Schools and Libraries." *American Library Association*, 29 Nov. 2021, www.ala.org/news/press-releases/2021/11/american-library-association-opposes-widespread-efforts-censor-books-us. Press release. Accessed 1 Oct. 2023.

Lebron, Sky. "DeSantis Calls Florida's Book Bans A 'Hoax,' Defends His Decision to Reject African American Course." Education, *WLRN*, 9 Mar. 2023, www. wlrn.org/education/2023-03-09/desantis-calls-floridas-book-bans-a-hoax-defends-his-decision-to-reject-african-american-course. Accessed 1 Nov. 2023 & 16 Jan. 2024

Lessenberry, Jack. "Plymouth-Canton School District Banning Books." *Michigan Public NPR,* 17 Jan. 2012, www.michiganradio.org/education/2012-01-17/plymouth-canton-school-district-banning-books. Accessed 19 Sept. 2023.

McKay, John. "Plymouth-Canton Parents, Teachers State Cases in Book Challenge." *Patch,* 12 Jan. 2012, updated 21 Jan. 2012, patch.com/michigan/plymouth-mi/parents-teachers-state-case-in-book-challenge. Accessed 18 Jan. 2024.

Michigan State. "Constitution of Michigan of 1835," *Michigan Legislature,* www.legislature.mi.gov/documents/historical/miconstitution1835.htm. Accessed 29 Oct. 2023, 1 Nov. 2023.

———. "Constitution of Michigan of 1850," *Michigan Legislature,* www.legislature.mi.gov/documents/historical/miconstitution1850.htm. Accessed 29 Oct. 2023, 1 Nov. 2023.

———. "Constitution of Michigan of 1963," *Michigan Legislature,* www.legislature.mi.gov/documents/mcl/pdf/mcl-chap1.pdf. Accessed 29 Oct. 2023, 1 Nov. 2023.

Morrison, Toni. *Beloved.* Penguin-Plume, 1988.

———. "Peril." *Burn This Book: PEN Writers Speak Out on the Power of the Word,* edited by Toni Morrison. HarperCollins, 2009, pp. 1–4.

———. "Rediscovering Black History." *What Moves at the Margin: Selected Nonfiction,* by Toni Morrison, edited by Carolyn C. Denard. UP of Mississippi, 2008, pp. 39–55.

"PEN America Index of School Book Bans—2021–2022." *PEN America,* 18 Apr. 2023, pen.org/banned-book-list-2021-2022/. Accessed 15 Sept. 2023

"The 1619 Project." *New York Time Magazine,* www.nytimes.com/interactive/2019/08/14/magazine/1619-america-slavery.html. Accessed 19 Sept. 2023, 17 Jan. 2024.

Updike, John. "Why Write?" Morrison, *Burn This Book,* pp. 5–21.

Waxman, Olivia B. "Why Toni Morrison's Books Are So Often the Target of Book Bans." *Time,* 31 Jan. 2022, time.com/6143127/toni-morrison-book-bans/. Accessed 1 Oct. 2023.

"WE CAN'T STOP LIVING"

No Love for Queer Memoirs in the Heartland

Haley M. Bateman and Patrick S. Allen

Book bans and challenges have proliferated in schools and libraries across the United States in the past year—and the scapegoats are familiar ones. Heated debates about what books should and should not be available to children and young adults are occurring online, at school board meetings, and in the courts. Works by people of color and queer authors have been disproportionately targeted and flagged for content deemed "inappropriate." PEN America, an organization dedicated to creative literary freedoms, calculated that 41 percent of banned books contain LGBTQ+ themes, and 40 percent have a protagonist of color (Friedman and Johnson). These targeted bans serve as a reminder for authors, readers, teachers, librarians, students, and activists alike that certain lives are continually deemed less "acceptable" or "appropriate" than others as minoritized groups and their literatures remain under attack in our schools and legislatures. Several midwestern states have emerged as an epicenter for this erasure, with contemporary queer memoirs like Alison Bechdel's *Fun Home* (2006), Maia Kobabe's *Gender Queer* (2019), and George M. Johnson's *All Boys Aren't Blue* (2020) having been challenged or banned in states including Missouri, Michigan, and Wisconsin ("Censorship"). Missouri Senate Bill 775 declares, "providing explicit sexual material to a student" a Class A misdemeanor, meaning a fine or jail time for librarians or teachers who do not comply with this ban (Missouri State). The 2022 bill, now law, has resulted in the removal of more than 300 books from classrooms, many of which do not align with the description in the bill, according to librarians and the ACLU (Farber).

The events of recent history can best be described, in our view, as a concerted silencing of queer and other marginalized voices across much of the Midwest. In a July 2023 letter to the nation's librarians, former US President Barack Obama wrote that "[i]t's no coincidence that these 'banned books' are often written by or feature people of color, indigenous people, and members of the LGBTQ+ community."

With an expulsion of queer texts at this scale, queer experiences, ideas, and histories are also being erased from the collective literary "archive," a collection or record of works that verifies the existence of someone or something.[1] Without an accessible record of these texts, they are effectively removed from the archive—or wholly denied a place therein—resulting in a gap, or an "archival silence."[2] These silences, and attempts at a wholesale silencing of LGBTQ+ individuals and culture today, threaten queer persons' erasure from the public eye, consequently leaving them more vulnerable to hostility and oppression.

Carmen Maria Machado addresses this silence and the process of erasure explicitly—on a personal and holistic level—in her 2019 memoir, *In the Dream House*. Machado's experience serves as a prescient warning about the nature of the archive and the processes by which its gatekeepers silence particular communities. Although Machado does not specifically address book bans in her memoir, we see this silencing playing out specifically in the current explosion of book bans and bills targeting works by LGBTQ+ authors. We posit that queer memoirs are so often erased because they actively resist the silences imposed upon them and aim to create and continually recreate a record lost or expunged. Machado's work—already banned in a Texas school district—is ripe for further challenges, and current, pending, and proposed legislation in several midwestern states suggests that such a move is not only likely but imminent.[3] Machado's desire to archive queer voices stems from her experience in an abusive relationship with another woman—whom she refers to as "the woman"—in Iowa and Indiana, placing her book at the center of our argument about queer memoirs and censorship thereof in the Heartland, and throughout the United States. She uses her memoir to explicitly challenge the erasure of queer people and their experiences from the record, as well as the attendant silence imposed upon them. She includes personal experience and scholarly research on queer theory and archives to provide a relatable and informative text for those who have survived or are currently experiencing domestic violence in a queer relationship, as well as those looking to learn about such ordeals. While Machado is focused primarily on the ways in which queer writers have historically avoided producing negative portrayals of queer persons and communities from within—an act of archival silence in itself—we explore here how her work's theories of the archive also offer critical modes of thinking about and challenging the silences imposed from without.

Archives and Silence

Machado's memoir offers the following dedication: "If you need this book, it is for you."[4] Her work thus simultaneously acknowledges the absence it seeks to fill and preempts challenges to come. *In the Dream House* provides a crucial and complex exploration of queer experiences and relationships, especially for those who "need" it. The memoir details Machado's experience with domestic abuse by another woman, giving readers insight into not only the forms such abuse can take but also the effects of such a tumultuous relationship, mental and physical. She manipulates point of view throughout the memoir—primarily using the second person—to bring the reader into the story and take them with her as her relationship spirals out of control. And she creates a dichotomy of "I" versus "You" to describe herself in and out of the relationship.[5] *Dream House* is a creative narrative that simultaneously interweaves scholarly research from and about archives and indexes, such as Saidiya Hartman's "Venus in Two Acts," Stith Thompson's *Motif Index of Folk-Literature*, and the Aarne-Thompson-Uther (ATU) Classification of Folk Tales to provide anecdotes, allegories, and historical references that may emphasize or illustrate particular points and that might resonate with readers of diverse literary and cultural milieux.[6]

Shortly after the two become an exclusive couple, Machado spends much of her time on the road and in Indiana with the woman rather than at her own home and in the community of the Iowa Writers' Workshop, the prestigious MFA program she was a part of at the University of Iowa. After being convinced to engage in a long-distance relationship and driving 408 miles from Iowa to Indiana consistently, she finds herself isolated in the woman's Bloomington residence—the eponymous "Dream House." She concurrently loses her voice in her relationship and her life, making an initial retelling of her story wearying and onerous. Machado begins a vignette titled "*Dream House as* Folktale Taxonomy" this way: "In Hans

Christian Andersen's story, the Little Mermaid has her tongue cut out of her head" (36).[7] The woman's stifling effect on Machado draws a connection between the author and the fairy-tale character, a stifling that is redoubled in the censorship of her book. At one point, after an early altercation, the woman tells Machado, "You're not allowed to write about this.... Don't you ever write about this. Do you fucking understand me?" (44). The ban in Texas—and those likely to follow—seems to repeat the woman's threat, with a difference: "You're not allowed to *read* about this." Of course, such silencing only makes the abuse more likely to continue. Scenes like this one, in which the woman threatens Machado should she speak up or speak out, exemplify the critical import of works like *Dream House* that offer readers a "toolbox" or a "reference guide" for identifying and naming abuse, or for resisting silence.

In a review of the memoir, Sharmila Mukherjee suggests that "Machado attributes her narrative predicament to an 'archival silence,' a [term] that poignantly captures the idea that certain histories—the history of queer domestic violence being one—never enter the cultural records; at best victims of such violence find themselves telling their stories in a vacuum or, at worst, they stay silent" (84). Many authors and survivors of domestic abuse end up suppressing their voices for various reasons. For queer folks, this silence is intensified by stigma. But we know, of course, from the woman's example, that this is precisely what the abuser wants. Machado urges her readers to combat this silencing, and she acts out this resistance by writing and publishing her memoir—that is, by entering it into the record. Mukherjee continues, "To make a coherent narrative in contextual 'silence,' Machado invents a language and a form to make her particular history legible" (84). The gaps in Machado's recollection of her traumatic relationship and her subsequent incorporation of existing literary devices and tropes create a text that combats archival erasures in multiple ways. She writes, "the nature of archival silence is that certain people's narratives and their nuances are swallowed by history; we see only what pokes through because it is sufficiently salacious for the majority to pay attention" (138). We add to Machado's critique of what never gets published the idea that book bans complete the job of swallowing up queer (hi)stories. Her memoir gives voice to her experience and allows it to be shared with queer youth, their families, and their allies to help them recognize abuse they may experience in their own lives, given the dearth of material on the topic.

Though Machado wrote from her own ordeal, she reiterates throughout her memoir that she found very little existing published material regarding abuse in queer relationships to validate her experiences (138–39, 245). Addressing this void, she argues, "Our culture does not have an investment in helping queer folks understand what their experiences *mean*" (139, italics in original). And this is precisely what book bans that target queer texts tell LGBTQ+ youth: your experiences are below the dignity of acknowledgment and analysis. Machado's understanding of the missing archive of queer domestic abuse, however, is not as simple as pointing out book bans or casting blame on publishers who refuse to (or simply do not) print queer texts. Instead, she recognizes that LGBTQ+ authors (and would-be authors) themselves have often opted not to record stories of abuse in the first place. Machado recalls thinking of the woman, who embodied rage issues and a personality disorder, "stop making us look bad" (126). And she recognizes in her own response what she calls a "minority anxiety" amongst queer authors who might worry that "if you're not careful, someone will see you—or people who share your identity—doing something human and use it against you" (228). This anxiety births self-censorship, which has, according to Machado, historically led queer authors to portray only the most respectable images of themselves and their LGBTQ+ characters.[8]

Such self-censorship speaks to the ubiquity and complexity of respectability politics within minoritized communities. In her 2017 book *Beyond Respectability*, Brittney C. Cooper describes respectability politics as simultaneously life-preserving and problematic. She contends that respectability has served as a strategy, particularly for Black women, "to navigate a hostile public sphere and to minimize the threat of sexual assault and other forms of bodily harm" (3), while recognizing that such politics are likewise a "complicated, contingent, and (rightfully) contested mode" of circumscribing identities worthy of respect (22). Machado returns to this idea of respectability throughout her memoir. She perhaps argues against self-censoring most clearly when she writes,

And it sounds terrible but it is, in fact, freeing: the idea that *queer* does not equal good or pure or right. It is simply a state of being—one subject to politics, to its own social forces, to larger narratives, to moral complexities of every kind. So bring on the queer villains, the queer heroes, the queer sidekicks and secondary characters and protagonists and extras. They can be a complete cast unto themselves. Let them have agency, and then let them go. (48, italics in original)

Machado dismantles the notion that only certain queer stories and persons should be represented in literature. And if we see this minority anxiety-induced self-censorship around respectability as an original filter that keeps certain queer stories from reaching readers, it appears that book bans attempt to sieve what does make it through.

Throughout her memoir, Machado directly invokes scholars such as José Esteban Muñoz and Saidiya Hartman to contextualize the forced silences she aims to bring to light. Machado quotes Muñoz's 2009 book *Cruising Utopia*, which, she writes, "pointed out that 'queerness has an especially vexed relationship to evidence…. When the historian of queer experience attempts to document a queer past, there is often a gatekeeper, representing a straight present'" (4). While she cuts the quote off at "present," Muñoz's sentence continues, "who will labor to invalidate the historical fact of queer lives—present, past, and future" (65). This reference to a straight gatekeeper who "invalidates" queer lives is precisely today's book banner. Reflecting on "What gets left behind?" Machado identifies "[g]aps where people never see themselves or find information about themselves. Holes that make it impossible to give oneself a context" (4–5). These missing elements prompt scholars like Hartman to turn to inferences to complete the unrecorded stories they seek to tell. Her seminal 2008 essay "Venus in Two Acts" confronts the notion that what is not entered into the official record does not matter or perhaps did not even occur. In a 2016 article that takes up similar questions of constructing stories from incomplete records, Hartman claims that the archive presents many difficulties "concern[ing] the forms of power and violence produced as historical fact; the silences, prolixities, and slippages" she encountered obscured the Middle Passage stories she was attempting to detail ("The Dead" 211). She continues, "The pathway to their [enslaved Africans'] thoughts was not one I could trace, but one I was required to imagine" (211). Broadened in context, Hartman's work reveals archives' limited information regarding all marginalized populations and the innovative methods scholars and artists must employ in recovering and narrativizing lost evidence. Both Hartman and Machado demonstrate that in order to work with the archives, one must also work "against" them to tell the whole story (Hartman, "Venus" 12; Machado 5). Even while writing her memoir, Machado seemingly expected attempts would be made to erase it. She writes, "Those who seek to silence queer voices and experiences will always find an excuse to remove them from archives and the public sector" (47), or to borrow Hartman's phase, to make them "asterisk[s] in the grand narrative of history" ("Venus" 2).

But silence need not always be figured negatively. J. Logan Smilges's 2022 book *Queer Silence* posits that, on the one hand, silence can represent an attempt to prevent queerness from entering the archive, while, on the other, it can be a self-chosen radical statement or a salvaging act. (We address this first concern here and return to the productive power of silence in the next section.) Smilges echoes Machado when addressing the results of removing queer experiences from the record: "Such limited representation is both a violence in itself as well as a justification for other violences.... Existing at the margins of the margins entails the threat of rhetorical erasure, leaving people voiceless among the invisible, unheard among the unseen" (Smilges 36). And that notion of "violence" is key. The laws, bills, and motions that aim to push queer people and their publications back into the closet are forms of state-sanctioned violence that do (and/or promote) real harm to real persons. For instance, Ohio House Bill 327 prohibits "teaching, advocating, or promoting divisive concepts" (Ohio State). Of course, in today's extremely polarized political climate, discussions addressing the very existence of LGBTQ+ people are being cast as "divisive," and thus persons must hide their identities or face repercussions. The language in the majority of book ban legislation is intentionally equivocal, allowing for anyone to effortlessly challenge texts that would recognize and benefit queer youth. Much like how Machado's voice was continually minimized until she had no footing in her relationship, efforts to ban queer memoirs and other creative works will continue until queer authors have no space in libraries, schools, or even bookshelves—if left unchecked. And therefore concerted resistance is necessary. Machado, like other queer authors and theorists, offers just such opposition. Recalling being stuck in a "Choose Your Own Adventure" loop of abuse, Machado reflects, "You have forgotten that leaving is an option" (177). Her memoir thus reminds readers that there is hope: abusers can be left; resources are available; queer voices will not be silenced.

Voicing the Silence(d)

As long as queer memoirs and experiences are at risk of erasure, queer authors will push to have their voices heard and recorded. Machado uses her memoir to "enter into the archive that domestic abuse between partners who share a gender identity is both possible and not uncommon" (5). *In the Dream House* combats silence, fills the gaps, and gives voice to those who have lost or not yet found their own. It shows queer youth that they are not alone. It gives proof to queer relationships in the Midwest, a region that is largely underrepresented in "mainstream" queer memoirs. For example, *Fun Home*, *Gender Queer*, and *All Boys Aren't Blue* are all centered on the East or West coasts of the United States. Growing up in the midwestern states can present its own unique set of challenges for LGBTQ+ youth. Researchers have found that LGBTQ+ adolescents in the midwestern, mountain, and southern states tend to be targeted, isolated, and pushed into the closet more often than their peers in regions with more inclusive curricula and legislatures (Hasenbush et al.; Karim et al.). Without legal protections in place and with current legislation increasingly targeting queer-inclusive curricula and literature, these youth are put at further risk. In fact, the Center for the Study of Hate and Extremism at California State University, San Bernardino, reports direct correlation between bans on gender-affirming care and books centering LGBTQ+ characters and a rise in anti-LGBTQ+ hate crimes. The increase has been so dramatic over the last year that hate crimes against queer people are the second most frequently occurring in the United States, behind race-based crimes (Levin).

Machado's memoir anticipates the effects of such legislation, like Florida's "Don't Say Gay" bill, signed into law in 2022. When her "scary aunt said, apropos of nothing, 'I don't believe in gay people,'" Machado identified a logical conclusion that stems from erasure: the belief that that which is erased indeed does not exist. She goes on to write, "and from the back seat—empowered by adulthood—you said, 'Well, we believe in you'" (71). Emboldened by her experience and age, Machado calls out her homophobic aunt (and perhaps homophobes en masse) in a moment that asserts queer people's existence and maybe even serves as a veiled threat. By mentioning her age, Machado likewise tells queer youth that it is okay if they do not yet feel capable of standing up to adult bullies, while perhaps also giving them permission to do so. Her witty comeback identifies an all-too-common sentiment, namely that queerness is not valid and necessitates correction. This belief that LGBTQ+ people do not exist and can be corrected or changed has staying power in the Midwest: only three midwestern states have full bans on conversion therapy ("Equality Maps"), and Wisconsin House Republicans recently voted to allow conversion therapy to continue in the state (Wirch). This culture creates an unsafe environment for LGBTQ+ youth in schools and communities. In her analysis of an ethnographic study of queer students and students of color in the Midwest, Boni Wozolek found that a majority of participants felt "unwelcome" and, in many cases, had experienced bullying by students and teachers as a result of their identities (277). Wozolek refers to a "hidden curriculum of violence," a phrase she uses as the title of her article to refer to the sexual violence and identity-based discrimination experienced by queer and POC students in schools. Such findings establish the necessity of having a record of queer experiences, for both queer and straight readers.

Though Machado's memoir confronts grim topics, it nonetheless gives LGBTQ+ youth a voice and presents them with an experience that can help them recognize that they are not alone, regardless of how their legislators, educators, and other people in their lives may contribute to their feelings of isolation. And it can likewise serve to humanize the queer community for readers who may have little experience with narratives about queer lives: that is, if they are allowed to read it. Machado addresses the conditions of her abuse and specifies how her split residence between Iowa and Indiana influenced her particular situation. She discusses how she lost her voice while living in the Dream House with the woman, and the way it isolated her from her family, friends, and peers. She writes, "you will learn that a common feature of domestic abuse is 'dislocation.' That is to say, the victim has just moved somewhere new, or she's somewhere where she doesn't speak the language, or has been otherwise uprooted from her support network, her friends or family, her ability to communicate. She is made vulnerable by her circumstance, her isolation" (72). Machado's vulnerability is heightened by this dislocation. Stuck in the Dream House with only her abuser, she is unable to find solace or safety. Notably, such an experience can be universal. Learning about dislocation gives any reader a tool for recognizing and understanding this feature of abuse should they experience or witness it in their own lives. In fact, across the globe, this phenomenon was exacerbated by COVID-19, and increases in domestic abuse have been documented following other dislocating events, such as natural disasters, when survivors of abuse had to remain with their abusers (Rauhaus et al. 668). The Dream House's location in Bloomington, where Machado had no close connections, compounds her discomfort and unfamiliarity, feelings which may be relatable to queer readers in similar midwestern settings.

In the Dream House thus provides LGBTQ+ adolescents with a "toolbox" or "guide" for identifying and naming domestic abuse in partnered relationships. Thinking of the memoir as a resource list is particularly meaningful if we share in Machado's realization about laws classifying abuse. The entirety of a vignette titled "*Dream House as* Epiphany" reads as follows: "Most types of domestic abuse are completely legal" (112). Returning to this point later in the memoir, Machado writes, "There is also the simple yet terrible fact that the legal system does not provide protection against most kinds of abuse—verbal, emotional, psychological— and even worse, it does not provide context" (138). The memoir, then, can be read as providing a series of examples that younger queer readers could use to identify, resist, and/or leave abusive situations in their own lives. It identifies the following as forms of abuse that may not always feel like abuse at all: touching you unlovingly (57); making demands about what you can say or write (44); pressuring you to do things you do not wish to (53); driving so recklessly you are terrified for your life (25–27, 87–90); twisting your words and gaslighting you (86; 98); forcing you to stop doing small things, like singing, that bring you joy (105); abandoning you in unfamiliar places (159); cyclically and repeatedly breaking up with you (114); and the list goes on, and on. When queer youth cannot learn about themselves in curricula, they turn to books for safety and experience, knowing someone can relate to them (Wexelbaum 112). By removing these books, school boards and legislatures are taking away outlets and resources for adolescents that may be their lifeline, their method of educating themselves on issues they are not being taught elsewhere (Kobabe; Wexelbaum 118). Banning such works means instilling a dangerous silence in the archive—one that leaves already-at-risk children even more vulnerable to abuse—making those who attempt these bans no better than the woman in the Dream House who repeatedly strives to prevent Machado from writing or speaking about her experience.

But despite the imperative of voicing queer experiences and making books about those experiences available to young people, sometimes silence is itself a strategy for survival. As indicated above, Smilges recognizes a positive use for queer silence and chooses to combat forced silences with intentional ones. They believe that queer silence can provide a safe space for LGBTQ+ persons to escape from their politicized identities. Much like an actualized version of "the closet," "[q]ueer silence promotes the kind of being differently together that allows marginalized folks across the board to take a break from their large-scale, structural organizing labor and, even if just for a few moments, settle into a little joy that we can have right now" (185). They discuss queer silence as a tool for queer liberation and posit that archival silence can be opposed by togetherness and solidarity between queer peoples. When queer people survive being silenced, they often aim to give voice to themselves and others who share similar experiences. Smilges tells the story of Dee Dee Ngozi, a trans woman who serves on the Mothers Board at her church and speaks for trans and other queer children whom she takes care of and are often left out of community conversations. By doing this, she enacts "a fungible fugitivity that sutures her traumas with others', knitting together a patchwork of silences into a quilt of radical kinship" (Smilges 163). A community is created amongst queer peo-ple who have been silenced; their collective voices converge resulting in something more powerful than the original—harmonic and boisterous solidarity. Whether by forcing themselves into the archive, fusing recorded and personal information, or creating unity, queer and other marginalized peoples continually find ways to resist book banning and to make their voices heard.

While Machado seeks to resist the archival silence imposed upon marginal-ized authors by documenting her experiences, Hartman draws from personal and familial experience to create complete and historically accurate narratives. She ex-hausted historical records, working with what she had and knew to inform and educate her audience. Today, her works serve as an extension of the official records and as a testament to the necessity of restoring lost voices. Her books are unlike any pre-existing historical records, because she used the hollow and foreboding silence of the archive to create something that encapsulates the experiences and presumed thoughts and feelings of people who lived through a largely undocu-mented event in history. Memoirs like Machado's that prompt discussion around "what counts" as a record serve a similar purpose to Hartman's work. *Dream House* posits that personal stories—even those without official documentation—matter to the archive. Scholars who focus their research on archival silences have named methods like Machado's, of crafting narratives from memory and from otherwise unrecorded or fragmented moments, "rebel" and "rogue" archives. Rather than uti-lizing conventional records, those who engage in sharing information from rebel and rogue archives "promote conversation around archival objects, rupturing the more prevalent model of solitary review that is commonplace at archival institu-tions" (Moss and Thomas 232). Through these processes, information can be shared and recorded without the perceived loneliness and emptiness of the record experienced by Hartman, Machado, and others. Through community-based, on-line, and other rebel and rogue approaches to sharing important scholarly, histor-ical, and cultural information, queer folks can continue to challenge the violence of archival erasure.

———————————

Notably, there has been some progress in the face of anti-LGBTQ+ bans in the Midwest. In June 2023, Illinois passed a law prohibiting book banning following sixty-seven attempted bans in the state in 2022. Governor J. B. Pritzker stated, "Young people shouldn't be kept from learning about the realities of our world.… Everyone deserves to see themselves reflected in the books they read, the art they see, the history they learn. In Illinois, we are showing the nation what it really looks like to stand up for liberty" ("Gov. Pritzker"). While this is a win for queer and marginalized representation, authors, scholars, and other citizens continue to push for other midwestern states to repeal their bans and emulate Illinois's efforts to protect queer voices.

In a *New York Times* op-ed addressing the banning of her book in Leander, Texas, Machado writes, "Those who seek to ban my book and others like it are trying to exploit fear—fear about the realities that books like mine expose, fear about desire and sex and love—and distort it into something ugly, in an attempt to wish away queer experiences" ("Book Bans"). Though it does not specifically mention bans, Machado's memoir serves as a reminder of the necessity to uplift and record queer voices and experiences. Her efforts to provide LGBTQ+ adolescents with a record of abuse in queer relationships, to critically reevaluate the self-censorship queer authors invoke to avoid negative portrayals, and to oppose outside attempts to silence or tone down queerness have not gone unnoticed. She has traversed the line between experience and archive, and her memoir's impact is a testimony to this. Like scholars such as Hartman and Smilges, she conveys the importance of the archive's role in creating space(s) for marginalized voices. Making such space necessitates continued efforts to combat book bans wherever and whenever they arise. *In the Dream House* makes the case that queerness is something to be espoused rather than erased. To those struggling to separate queer rights from queer morality, Machado offers this: "*We can't stop living.* Which means *we have to live*, which means *we are alive*, which means *we are humans and we are human*" (48, italics in original).

Elizabethtown College

Notes

1. Throughout this article, we use "archive" and "record" interchangeably to refer to this collection of materials and stories.

2. For scholarship on and definitions of "archival silence" see Klein; Manoff; and Thomas et al., particularly chapters 1 and 4.

3. Legislation introduced in midwestern states includes Michigan House Bill 4136 and Wisconsin Senate Bill 10, which restrict access to "obscene" or "harmful" material in public libraries and schools (Michigan State; Wisconsin State). Laws passed include Iowa Senate File 496, which bans books with descriptions of sex acts and prohibits instruction on gender identity or sexual orientation before seventh grade (Iowa State), and Indiana House Bill 1447 that allows parents and community members to request books be banned from school libraries that they deem "obscene" or "harmful to minors" (Indiana State).

4. Unless otherwise noted, all references to Machado come from *In the Dream House*.

5. Prudence Bussey-Chamberlain discusses Machado's experimental approach to portraying queer abuse, especially through her use of numerous literary devices in the memoir. She writes, "This is reflected in the shifting subject, who sometimes takes the form of a present day 'I,' with the benefit of hindsight, but is mostly comprised of a second person 'you.' This serves to highlight Machados' [sic] temporal distance from the events of the book, but also enacts the immediate and aftereffects of trauma rupturing a self to the point of double existence: the 'you' who endured abuse, and the embodied self, 'I,' that coexists with this violence" (260).

6. Machado's broader references range from Disney films to the poetry of Sappho and from the classic 1944 film *Gaslight* to the genre of the American gothic, thus opening doors for readers to connect to the material via any number of paths. Moreover, in her Afterword, Machado offers a list of more than twenty-five books and other resources for readers interested in further exploring the memoir's themes.

7. All but one of the memoir's chapters are titled "*Dream House as…*," where a genre, event, or theme completes the title. The one exception is a particularly experimental chapter in which Machado does not permit herself to use the letter "e," so she borrows a German term, titling that chapter "*Traumhaus as Lipogram*" (149).

8. While we generally agree with Machado's assertion, we recognize that there are notable exceptions. For example, James Baldwin's classic 1956 novel *Giovanni's Room* centers on a cast of rather unlikable and even abusive queer characters. Baldwin's characters are men, however, which illustrates Machado's claims elsewhere in the memoir that women are rarely cast as abusers in LGBTQ+ literature. See the chapter "*Dream House as* Ambiguity" for an in-depth discussion of this gendered difference (135–39).

Works Cited

Bussey-Chamberlain, Prudence. "'Every Lover Is a Destroyer': Queer Abuse and Experimental Memoir in Melissa Febos' *Abandon Me* and Carmen Maria Machado's *In the Dream House*." *Prose Studies*, vol. 42, no. 3, 2021, pp. 259–78, doi.org/10.1080/01440357.2022.2144081.

"Censorship by the Numbers." *American Library Association*, 2023, www.ala.org/advocacy/bbooks/by-the-numbers.

Cooper, Brittney C. *Beyond Respectability: The Intellectual Thought of Race Women.* U of Illinois P, 2017, www.jstor.org/stable/10.5406/j.ctt1q31sfr.

"Equality Maps: Conversion 'Therapy' Laws." *Movement Advancement Project*, 16 Aug. 2023, www.lgbtmap.org/equality-maps/conversion_therapy.

Farber, Alicja. "Missouri ACLU Sues on Behalf of Library Associations Over Book-Ban Law." *The Free Speech Project*, Georgetown University, 17 Apr. 2023, freespeechproject.georgetown.edu/tracker-entries/missouri-aclu-sues-on-behalf-of-library-associations-over-book-ban-law/.

Friedman, Jonathan, and Nadine Farid Johnson. "Banned in the USA: The Growing Movement to Censor Books in Schools." *PEN America*, 22 Sept. 2022, pen.org/report/banned-usa-growing-movement-to-censor-books-in-schools/.

"Gov. Pritzker Signs Bill Making Illinois First State in the Nation to Outlaw Book Bans." *Illinois.gov*, 12 June 2023, www.illinois.gov/news/press-release.26575. html. Press release.

Hartman, Saidiya. "The Dead Book Revisited." *History of the Present*, vol. 6, no. 2, 2016, pp. 208–15, doi.org/10.5406/historypresent.6.2.0208.

———. "Venus in Two Acts." *Small Axe*, vol. 12, no. 2, 2008, pp. 1–14, doi. org/10.1215/-12-2-1.

Hasenbush, Amira, et al. "The LGBT Divide: A Data Portrait of LGBT People in the Midwest, Mountain, and Southern States." *The Williams Institute*, Dec. 2014, williamsinstitute.law.ucla.edu/lgbtdivide/#.

Indiana State, Congress, House, Committee on Education and Career Development. HB 1447: Education Matters. *Legiscan.com*, 4 May 2023, legiscan.com/IN/ bill/HB1447/2023. Public Law 234.

Iowa State, Congress, Senate, Education Committee. Senate File 496: Act Relating to Children and Students. *Bill Track 50*, 26 May 2023, www.billtrack50.com/ billdetail/1589681. 90th General Assembly.

Karim, Sana, et al. "Support over Social Media among Socially Isolated Sexual and Gender Minority Youth in Rural U.S. during the COVID-19 Pandemic: Opportunities for Intervention Research." *International Journal of Environmental Research and Public Health*, vol. 19, no. 23, 2022, doi.org/10.3390/ ijerph192315611.

Klein, Lauren F. "The Image of Absence: Archival Silence, Data Visualization, and James Hemings." *American Literature*, vol. 85, no. 4, 2013, pp. 661–88, doi. org/10.1215/00029831-2367310.

Kobabe, Maia. "Schools Are Banning My Book. But Queer Kids Need Queer Stories." *The Washington Post*, 29 Oct. 2021, www.washingtonpost.com/ opinions/2021/10/29/schools-are-banning-my-book-queer-kids-need- queer-stories/. Opinion.

Levin, Brian. Interview with Leila Fadel. "Hate Crimes in the Nation's 10 Largest Cities Spiked Significantly Last Year." *NPR Morning Edition*, 18 Sept. 2023, www.npr.org/2023/09/18/1200076895/hate-crimes-in-the-nations-10-largest-cities-spiked-significantly-last-year.

Machado, Carmen Maria. "Banning My Book Won't Protect Your Child." *The New York Times*, 11 May 2021, www.nytimes.com/2021/05/11/opinion/censorship-domestic-violence-book.html. Opinion.

———. *In the Dream House: A Memoir*. Graywolf Press, 2019.

Manoff, Marlene. "Mapping Archival Silence: Technology and the Historical Record." *Engaging with Records and Archives: Histories and Theories*, edited by Fiorella Foscarini et al., Facet, 2016, pp. 63–82, doi.org/10.29085/9781783301607.005.

Michigan State, Congress, House, Committee on Local Government and Municipal Finance. HB 4136 The Library Privacy Act. *Legisture.mi.gov*, 22 Feb. 2023, www.legislature.mi.gov/documents/2023-2024/billintroduced/House/pdf/2023-HIB-4136.pdf.

Missouri State, Congress, Senate, Judiciary and Civil and Criminal Jurisprudence Committee. SB 775 Modifies Provisions Relating to Judicial Proceedings. *Senate.mo.gov*, 28 Aug. 2022, www.senate.mo.gov/22info/pdf-bill/tat/SB775.pdf. 101st General Assembly, Second Session.

Moss, Michael, and David Thomas. *Archival Silences: Missing, Lost, and Uncreated Archives*, Routledge, 2021, doi.org/10.4324/9781003003618.

Mukherjee, Sharmila. Review of Carmen Maria Machado's *In the Dream House: A Memoir*. *World Literature Today*, vol. 94, no. 2, 2020, p. 84, doi.org/10.1353/wlt.2020.0152.

Muñoz, José Esteban. "Gesture, Ephemera, and Queer Feeling: Approaching Kevin Aviance." *Cruising Utopia: The Then and There of Queer Futurity*, New York UP, 2009, pp. 65–89.

Obama, Barack. Letter to American librarians. *Twitter*, 17 July 2023, 9:10 a.m., twitter.com/BarackObama/status/1680927869021696005/photo/1.

Ohio State, Congress, House of Representatives. House Bill 327 As Introduced. *The Ohio Legislature*, 2022, search-prod.lis.state.oh.us/solarapi/v1/general_ assembly_134/bills/hb327/IN/00/hb327_00_IN?format=pdf.   134th General Assembly, Regular Session, 2021–2022.

Rauhaus, Beth M., et al. "Addressing the Increase of Domestic Violence and Abuse During the COVID-19 Pandemic: A Need for Empathy, Care, and Social Equity in Collaborative Planning and Responses." *The American Review of Public Administration*, vol. 50, no. 6–7, 2020, pp. 668–74, doi. org/10.1177/0275074020942079.

Smilges, J. Logan. *Queer Silence: On Disability and Rhetorical Absence*. U of Minnesota P, 2022.

Thomas, David, et al. *The Silence of the Archive*. Facet, 2017.

Wexelbaum, Rachel. "The Reading Habits and Preferences of LGBTIQ+ Youth." *The International Journal of Information, Diversity, & Inclusion*, vol. 3, no. 1, Jan. 2019, pp. 112–29, www.jstor.org/stable/48644501.

Wirch, Robert. "Denying the Chance for Public Input, Republicans Reaffirm Support for 'Conversion Therapy' During Pride Month." *Wisconsin State Legislature*, District 22, 2023, legis.wisconsin.gov/senate/22/wirch/press/ denying-the-chance-for-public-input-republicans-reaffirm-support-for- conversion-therapy-during-pride-month/. Press release.

Wisconsin State, Senate, Committee on Mental Health, Substance Abuse Prevention, Children and Families. Senate Bill 10: Pupil or Minor Access to Harmful Material in Public Libraries and to Harmful Material or Offensive Material in Public Schools. *Legiscan.com*, 21 Feb. 2023, legiscan.com/WI/text/ SB10/2023.

Wozolek, Boni. "Hidden Curriculum of Violence: Affect, Power, and Policing the Body." *Educational Studies*, vol. 56, no. 3, 2020, pp. 269–85, doi.org/10.1080/ 00131946.2020.1745808.

LITERARY GATEKEEPING IN MIDWESTERN CLASSROOMS
Book Challenges, Early Reading Instruction,
and Reading in Context

Patricia Oman

In Fall 2022, in response to recent nationwide efforts to remove books from public K-12 classrooms and libraries, I taught a course on banned books. The focus was not just on the books themselves, but also on the gatekeepers between literature and young readers: parents, librarians, educators, school boards, and other people who decide what young people in the United States should and should not read. I had practical reasons for developing this course—as future middle school and high school teachers, the English Education majors in my department are worried about stepping into the classroom in the midst of recent book challenges and new state legislation prohibiting certain topics and classroom materials. In this essay I draw on the good discussions and debates in that class to offer practical advice to English and Language Arts educators facing challenges to the books they teach.

In the first section, I explore the connections among current book challenges; debates about methods of early reading instruction, particularly whole-language learning; and the recent classical charter school movement. I argue that book challenges today are part of a larger political effort not just to control the books available to young readers but also to limit reading literature in its cultural and historical context, to define literacy as ahistorical and apolitical. In the next two sections I demonstrate through case studies of two midwestern texts—Toni Morrison's 1970 novel *The Bluest Eye* and Henry Wadsworth Longfellow's 1855 poem *Song of Hiawatha*—that educational practices such as reading instruction and literary canon formation *are* political and that literature should be read in its cultural and historical contexts. Finally, I give practical advice to English and Language Arts educators about book challenges.

Book Challenges Today

The phenomenon of book challenges is not new in the United States. The uniqueness of our current cultural and historical moment is the *degree* to which parents and political organizations are challenging books in public K-12 schools and public libraries. The American Library Association (ALA) documented 1,269 book challenges in the United States in 2022, compared with 729 book challenges in 2021 (Garcia). PEN America documented 3,362 book challenges in the 2022–23 school year, compared with 2,532 in the 2021–22 school year (Meehan et al.) The coordination of these challenges by a small group of people can be seen in a number of studies. Of the 1,269 book challenges in 2022, for example, the ALA found that "90% were part of attempts to censor multiple titles" (Garcia). In fact, 40% of books challenged in 2022 were part of "cases involving 100 or more books" ("Book Ban Data"). In a study of more than 986 book challenges in the 2021–22 academic year, *The Washington Post* found that 60% of all challenges nationwide came from just eleven people who had each filed more than ten challenges, while another 25% of challenges came from people who had filed between two and nine challenges (Natanson).

Organizations such as Moms for Liberty, Citizens Defending Freedom, and Parents' Rights in Education show that book challenges today are related to the small but vocal "Parents Rights" movement, a post-COVID effort that aims to prevent so-called woke indoctrination of children in schools. Tiffany Justice, cofounder of Moms for Liberty, for example, says in a video on the organization's website, "[The cofounders of Moms for Liberty] both served as school board members, and we saw behind the education curtain. And then COVID happened, and all of America saw behind the education curtain. We're about parental rights. Every parent has a fundamental right to direct the upbringing of their children, their medical care, their healthcare, their education. We do not coparent with the government" ("We Are Winning"). Images in the video demonstrate that this effort for parental rights includes challenging books. For this organization, fighting for parental rights is no less than "fighting for the survival of America" ("Who We Are").

Spurred on by these organizations, Parents Rights bills that attempt to expand parental control over public education, including issues related to children's gender identities and curricular materials in public schools and libraries, have been introduced in many states. Bella DiMarco of Future Ed.org tracked eighty-five such bills introduced in twenty-six states in 2022 and sixty-two bills introduced in twenty-four states in 2023. A federal Parents Rights bill passed the US House of Representatives in March 2023 but has not been discussed in the Senate. Book challenges, therefore, are just one part of this political movement. In this essay I want to consider book challenges alongside two related trends in education: (1) growing support for a method of early reading instruction called the "science of reading" and (2) networks of classical charter schools that directly challenge the curricula (and funding) of mainstream public schools.

Methods for teaching reading throughout the twentieth and twenty-first centuries have waffled between versions of a phonics approach, which teach early readers to recognize graphemes and phonemes (the "sound it out" method), and versions of the "whole language" approach, which teach early readers to memorize words and use context to understand meaning (the "look-say" method). Proponents of the former method view reading as a taught skill, whereas proponents of the latter method view reading as a natural extension of language acquisition. The "science of reading" approach, which encourages teaching reading as a decoding skill, that is, a return to phonics instruction, has wide bipartisan support today, but the endorsement of the method by Moms for Liberty suggests the method is not without ideological implications. In an October 2023 interview with *Education Week*, cofounder Justice made an explicit link between the "science of reading" and removing diverse texts from the classroom, arguing, "The idea that there's more emphasis placed on diversity in the classroom, rather than teaching kids to read, is alarming at best. That's criminal" (Schwartz). As the author of the article, Sarah Schwartz, notes, "pitting basic skills against culturally responsive practices is a false dichotomy," but Justice sees the ideological potential of a phonics approach.

Lack of clarity seems to be part of whole language's history, but it consistently emphasizes the importance of reading in context. In 1987 Bess Altwerger, Carole

Edelsky, and Barbara M. Flores gave this definition of whole language in the journal *The Reading Teacher:*

> Whole language is *not* practice. It is a set of beliefs, a perspective…. based on
> the following ideas: (a) language is for making meanings, for accomplishing
> purposes; (b) written language is language—thus what is true for language
> in general is true for written language; (c) the cuing systems of language
> (phonology in oral, orthography in written language, morphology, syntax,
> semantics, pragmatics) are always simultaneously present and interacting
> in any instance of language in use; (d) language use always occurs in a situa-
> tion; (e) situations are critical to meaning-making. (145, italics in original)

Altwerger et al.'s description does not ignore the decoding (i.e., phonics) aspects of language (phonology, orthography, morphology, syntax, etc.), as many detrac-tors claim, but whole language *does* emphasize that context is important for reading comprehension (i.e., reading does not happen in a linguistic or cultural vacuum) and that the rhetorical situation of language or text contributes to its meaning. The authors note that in practice this often means that students perform "real reading and writing, not exercises in reading and writing," and "rel[y] heavily on literature, on other print used for appropriate purposes (e.g., cake mix directions used for re-ally making a cake rather than for finding short vowels), and on writing for varied purposes" (145). Thus, however effective it may or may not be as a method of early reading instruction, the whole-language approach nevertheless emphasizes import-ant aspects of reading comprehension.

In the 1990s, whole-language instruction correlated with both an increase in diverse books for children and an increased use of whole works of literature (i.e., tradebooks) over basal readers in elementary classrooms. (Basal readers are de-signed by publishers specifically for reading instruction and up until the 1990s typ-ically included short passages or excerpts rather than whole works.) In their 2000 survey of research on the use of children's literature in reading instruction, Miriam G. Martinez and Lea M. McGee summarize a 1998 national survey in which 72%

of prekindergarten to fifth-grade teachers reported using primarily tradebooks to teach and/or encourage reading (159). The authors note, "The results of this survey reveal a very different picture than that of earlier decades in which the use of basal readers accounted for between 90 and 95% of all reading instruction in U.S. elementary schools" (160). While it is impossible to find direct causation for the increased use of tradebooks in early reading instruction, Martinez and McGee cite multiple contributing trends, among them, teacher-led movements (such as whole language), scholarly reconception of literacy and literature in literacy journals, and a boom in publishing for children (159–65). They note that about 5,000 tradebooks for children were published annually in the 1990s, compared to approximately 2,000 children's books published annually in the 1960s, and by 2000 there were over 70,000 children's books in print (161). Martinez and McGee note that publishing trends in children's literature of the 1980s and 1990s included "[a] notable increase in multicultural literature," arguing specifically that "[e]ducators involved in both the whole language and literature-based reading movements have recognized the importance of reading materials relevant to children's lives and have sought out multicultural literature for use in their literacy programs" (162).

While whole-language reading instruction encompasses a wide set of practices, today the method is associated with diversity and multiculturalism. This is likely due, in part, to the co-trends of assigning whole works of literature and the increase in diverse children's literature published in the 1990s. But it is also due to the explicit connection of whole language today to issues like social justice. Literacies and Languages for All (LLA), formerly called Whole Language Umbrella, is a group of the National Council of Teachers of English that promotes whole-language learning today, referring to it as "holistic" education. Their website notes that members "believe that ALL children deserve personally meaningful learning contexts in which their languages and cultures are valued and recognized as assets for learning." Members of this group "integrate theories and practices of social justice; critical literacies; digital, multimodal, and biliteracies; and inquiry- and project-based learning that embody the work of 21st-century educators" ("Literacies and Languages"). Reading and writing in context are imagined by this group as composing for new and multiple modalities and reading and writing with awareness of cultural contexts. While "practices of social justice" are not a logical extension of the "look-say" method of reading by itself, they are a logical extension of whole language's emphasis on reading in context. It is reasonable, therefore, that some might interpret the popularity of the "science of reading" as a move away from diversity of reading content.

I have no opinion on the debates between teaching phonics or teaching whole language in early reading instruction—I will leave early reading instruction to early reading specialists—but I do think it is important to clarify a few conceptual binaries that seem to get lumped together in debates about reading instruction and literature. First, it is important to separate the "look-say" reading method of whole-language instruction from the many culturally sensitive practices that became associated with it in the 1980s and 1990s. Groups such as Moms for Liberty *and* Literacies and Languages for All apparently conflate the reading method with diversity. Second, the debate between phonics and whole-language instruction boils down to a debate between *denotative* and *connotative* meaning. Phonics approaches focus on decoding graphemes and phonemes to process written language, that is, learning the direct correlation between signifiers and their signifieds, whereas whole-language methods focus on the whole sign, the signifier and its many potential signifieds. *Both* denotative and connotative meaning are important for reading comprehension, though. Third, the debate about basal readers and whole literature is a similar binary of denotative and connotative meaning. Basal readers give readers passages and excerpts out of context, encouraging severely limited connotative skills, whereas whole works of literature allow readers to understand passages in context.

The recent rise in charter schools that focus on so-called classical education or Great Books is a corollary to book challenges and debates about early reading instruction because of the way Great Books curricula limit possibilities for reading in context. The prescribed curriculum for high school students at Valor Classical Schools in Texas, for example, includes many classical western authors, including Homer, Herodotus, Sophocles, Plato, and Virgil. In the 9th grade, students read several canonical American authors, such as Nathaniel Hawthorne, Mark Twain, Henry David Thoreau, Ralph Waldo Emerson, and even Booker T. Washington, W. E. B. DuBois, and Martin Luther King, Jr. ("Integrated Humanities Program"). Great Hearts Academies, a chain of online and in-person schools dedicated to the "pursuit of Truth, Goodness, and Beauty," includes a similar mix of ancient and traditional American authors ("Home"; "High School Reading List"). I do not think a classical or Great Books education is bad—my own high school and undergraduate education was highly steeped in Latin and Greek and the so-called Great Books of western literature—but the curriculum seems to actively discourage reading contemporary literary texts *and* reading literary texts in their contemporaneous contexts. Instead, students are given a particular narrative, "Truth, Goodness, and Beauty," or what Matthew Arnold would call "sweetness and light," from which to create meaning.

These charter schools' focus on the western and American literary canons is both traditional and politically motivated. The tension between a unified or homogeneous national identity and more "diverse" authors is the center of many debates about the American literary canon and what texts should be taught in classrooms. Excluding contemporary and multiethnic books from the classroom is an ideologically motivated decision to exclude ideas that challenge the status quo. In the introduction to the edited collection *Multiethnic American Literatures*, for example, Helane Adams Androne argues,

> Because [multiethnic] literatures force our serious examination of the assumptions of privilege, equal citizenship and justice, and sometimes call up raw and intense experiences from the liminal spaces that rapidly growing minority and academically marginalized populations occupy, these texts find themselves flying in the face of the idealism of mobility, universality of privilege, and absence of persistently restrictive systems modeled in much of the literature in the canon. Instead, many of the texts that question these limits end up on "banned" lists in many educational systems, available only to the persistent after activism or approval. (3)

Book challenges are probably not an issue at these classical charter schools because they have already excluded the types of books that are being challenged in public schools and public libraries around the country.

Many book challenges today boil down to restricting connotative meaning. In fact, the common reasons given for book challenges today suggest systematic and willful attempts to read literature out of context, out of the context of the literary work as a whole and out of the work's cultural context. PEN America notes that in the 3,362 book bans it tracked in the 2022–23 school year, 48% of challenged books include violence or abuse, 42% cover topics "on health and wellbeing for students," 33% detail sexual experiences, 30% "include characters of color or discuss race and racism," and 30% include LGBTQ+ characters or themes (Meehan et al.). These statistics do not acknowledge how these themes are presented in each book, however. Further, that these book challenges are trying to limit children's exposure to reading literature that addresses its contemporaneous context can be seen in the close association of challenges with LGBTQ content and racial diversity. When asked by *The Washington Post* to analyze book challenges to LGBTQ content, for example, the ALA found that the percentage of challenges to LGBTQ content has risen sharply in the last two decades. "From the 2000s to the early 2010s," Hannah Natanson writes, "LGBTQ books were the targets of between less than 1 and 3 percent of book challenges filed in schools," but "[t]hat number rose to 16 percent by 2018, 20 percent in 2020 and 45.5 percent in 2022."

My purpose in looking at book challenges, debates about early reading instruction, and the literary canon together is to note that literacy and worldview are closely connected. Recent educational trends such as book challenges, the "science of reading," and classical charter schools are thus attempts to restrict young people's worldviews. The following sections analyze examples of whole-language instruction in the early twentieth century: William Elson and William Gray's Dick and Jane Basic Readers (as critiqued in Morrison's *The Bluest Eye*) and Florence Holbrook's 1898 *The Hiawatha Primer* (a whole-language textbook inspired by Longfellow's *Song of Hiawatha*). These examples show that whole-language instruction is not inherently connected to diversity but that literacy *is* political.

Literacy and Marginalization in The Bluest Eye

Toni Morrison's 1970 novel *The Bluest Eye*, which has been one of the most challenged books in the United States since its publication, is a good case study for the ideological implications of debates about book challenges, early reading instruction, and the literary canon. Set in northern Ohio in the early 1940s, the novel addresses the psychological effects of institutional and educational racism on Black children through the story of eleven-year-old Pecola Breedlove. The book is number three on the American Library Association's list of most challenged books of 2022 because of "depiction of sexual abuse, [DEI] content" and because it is "claimed to be sexually explicit" ("Top 13 Most Challenged Books"). According to the ALA, it was the tenth most challenged book in the United States in 2010–19, the fifteenth in 2000–09, and the thirty-fourth in 1990–99 ("100 Most, 1990"; "100 Most, 2000"; "100 Most, 2010"). To be clear, the book does not promote sexual abuse or call for racial divisiveness; rather, it suggests that the sexual abuse and racism described in the novel are products, in part, of American popular culture and American educational practices. In particular, the book implicates William Elson and William Gray's Dick and Jane Basic Readers series in helping to perpetuate institutional racism in the United States.

The novel's title, *The Bluest Eye*, comes from Pecola's belief that her life would be better if she were white and had blond hair and blue eyes. Her obsession with beautiful white girls in American popular culture reveals the absence of models of Black female beauty in mainstream culture in the 1930s and 1940s. The reactions of another character, nine-year-old Claudia MacTeer, to the same images show why these seemingly innocent images can have traumatic consequences for young Black girls. When Pecola spends a long time "gaz[ing] fondly at ... Shirley Temple," for example, Claudia thinks about how much she hates Shirley, "[n]ot because she was cute, but because she danced with Bojangles, who was *my* friend, *my* uncle, *my* daddy, and who ought to have been soft-shoeing it and chuckling it with me" (19, italics in original). At the age of nine, Claudia intuitively recognizes the cultural appropriation of a Black performer, Bill "Bojangles" Robinson, for white audiences and refuses to approve of the young white performer who benefits from his tutelage.

The Bluest Eye demonstrates in fictional form the effects of what W. E. B. Du-Bois calls in his 1903 book *The Souls of Black Folk* "double consciousness." DuBois describes the experience of being Black in America as "a sense of always looking at one's self through the eyes of others, of measuring one's soul by the tape of a world that looks on in amused contempt and pity. One ever feels his two-ness,—an American, a Negro; two souls, two thoughts, two unreconciled strivings; two warring ideals in one dark body, whose dogged strength alone keeps it from being torn asunder" (3). Double consciousness is essentially the recognition of conflicting denotative meanings, the meaning attributed to Black bodies by white culture and the meaning attributed to them by Black culture. Evelyn Jaffe Schreiber argues that by using the concept of double consciousness *The Bluest Eye* "reenact[s] the white constructions of beauty, order, and family to illustrate how the imposition of these standards on blacks prevents the development of a black identity based on African American cultural ritual" (83). Pecola, who lacks any psychic defenses, experiences literal double consciousness by the end of the novel, her selfhood split into two different personalities arguing with each other (204). The novel makes it impossible for readers to miss the point that Pecola's psychological breakdown is partly the result of a hegemonic white culture that denotatively associates beautiful girls with blue eyes. Her disassociation is caused by both the trauma of sexual abuse and the trauma of a culture that implicitly denotes her as ugly and unlovable. The novel thus shows what DuBois's theory of double consciousness looks like in practice (i.e., in context).

While Pecola's example is extreme, double consciousness affects even Claudia and her older sister Frieda, who have the support of a stable, loving family. When she is young, Claudia defies white standards of beauty by rejecting the "white baby dolls" she receives at Christmas. "Adults, older girls, shops, magazines, newspapers, window signs—all the world," she narrates, "had agreed that a blue-eyed, yellow-haired, pink-skinned doll was what every girl child treasured" (20). Claudia dismembers these dolls, however, until she learns how "repulsive this disinterested violence" is and hides it in "love" (23). Like Frieda and Pecola, Claudia eventually comes to love Shirley Temple as a necessary and unifying step in her psychological development, but that development means accepting standards of beauty and ugliness imposed by white culture. In other words, it means accepting the association between the signifiers *white skin* and *blue eyes* and the hegemonic culture's meaning—beauty. Unfortunately for Claudia, who does not have white skin or blue eyes, this compliance comes with a large dose of unconscious self-hatred.

While popular culture bears much of the responsibility for Pecola's psychological breakdown, *The Bluest Eye* also explores the psychological effects of institutional education on the Black children of the novel. Morrison's inclusion of William Elson and William Gray's popular Dick and Jane Basic Readers in the novel implicates the ideological role of reading instruction in Pecola's psychological breakdown. Debra T. Werrlein, for example, writes that though "Elson and Gray produced the Basic Readers to promote literacy, not specifically to propagate destructive ideologies," they nevertheless "point to who they expected to educate—who they envisioned as the nation's future citizens" (62). Based on the content and images of the books, those assumed readers (and future citizens) were the children of white, suburban, nuclear families.

The emphasis on children in *The Bluest Eye* is especially interesting given the recent introduction of Parents Rights bills in the United States. The efforts of groups like Moms for Liberty to "save America" by safeguarding the innocence of children demonstrates the discursive connection between "children" and "America" in these movements. Werrlein argues that *The Bluest Eye* addresses this discursive tendency in American culture. Reading *The Bluest Eye* as a product of the reactionary period after the Civil Rights era, she writes, "[W]hen 1970s America had already begun to assemble nostalgic myths about suburban life during and after World War II, Morrison focuses on family, education, and popular culture to expose childhood innocence as a pervasive ideology that simultaneously perpetuates and mystifies the harsher realities of white nationalist hegemony" (Werrlein 56). In other words, Morrison's point, according to Werrlein, is to reveal the concept of childhood innocence as an ideological construct in American culture that perpetuates white privilege and dominance. Werrlein might interpret book challenges today that aim to protect children from so-called dangerous ideas, like those in the frequently challenged *The Bluest Eye*, in a similar light.

It is important to note, however, that Morrison's critique of the Dick and Jane Basic Readers is a critique of the uncritical application of whole-language reading instruction. The first section of the novel, for example, begins with a paragraph of text from a typical Dick and Jane reader: "Here is the house. It is green and white. It has a red door. It is very pretty. Here is the family.…" (3). The text is repeated in the next paragraph, but without punctuation or capital letters: Here is the pretty house it is green and white it has a red door it is very pretty here is the family …" (4). In the third, and final, paragraph of the section, the text is repeated again, this time without any punctuation, capital letters, or spacing between words: "Hereisthe-houseitisgreenandwhiteithasareddooritisveryprettyhereisthefamily …" (4). The first paragraph demonstrates the method of whole-language instruction, in which early readers are exposed to a few words at a time and learn to memorize them so that they can eventually read fluently, without having to sound out every word. Morrison's revision of the paragraph, erasing all the markers that allow readers to distinguish between the words, accomplishes two goals. On one hand, the words are made strange and unfamiliar through the repetition and deletion of spaces. De-familiarizing concepts like beauty is the goal of the novel so that readers can recognize them as constructed. On the other hand, the repetitions show how words and concepts become internalized in whole-language instruction.

While Werrlein argues that *The Bluest Eye* implies that "from their inception, Elson-Gray primers participated in a national illiteracy campaign that systematically disenfranchised young black Americans, especially young black girls" (62), I think it is important to clarify exactly how that happens at the level of reading. Whole-language instruction relies on both memorizing and contextualizing words. When young readers see the word *family* in the Dick and Jane books, they make a connotative association between the image of the word and the image of the nuclear family on the page. Morrison's implicit critique of this method of reading is actually the slippage between denotative and connotative meaning. If young readers are able to associate the word-image *family* only with a white nuclear family, the association necessarily becomes *denotative*. The memorization of the word through repetition in the whole-language method reinscribes this denotative meaning until it seems fluent and natural. The pairing of the Dick and Jane Basic Readers with popular cultural artifacts such as Shirley Temple, Mary Jane candies, the film *Imitation of Life*, and white baby dolls in the novel reinforces the denotative association of *beauty* with white skin, blond hair, and blue eyes in American culture.

Morrison might agree with the problematic nature of whole-language instruction in the Dick and Jane books, but she would not agree with moving away from diverse literature. *The Bluest Eye* is one of those multicultural texts that Androne argues flies "in the face of the idealism of mobility" and the "universality of privilege" (3). Those who challenge the novel today because of its depiction of child sexual abuse and incest willfully ignore both the context of the sexual abuse and incest in the novel and the cultural contexts of the novel's setting and writing. Further, removing the book from classrooms and libraries discourages students from examining the ideological implications of the educational system through which they became literate.

The Hiawatha Primer *and* The Song of Hiawatha
in Context

A staple of American schools in the late nineteenth and early twentieth centuries, Henry Wadsworth Longfellow's 1855 poem *The Song of Hiawatha* is an American epic poem, Longfellow's attempt "to author a national American narrative" (Nurmi 254). Set on the southern shore of Lake Superior, the poem depicts the adventures of Ojibwe warrior Hiawatha and his love for the Dakota woman Minnehaha (Longfellow 207). It was wildly popular upon publication, and its regular trochaic tetrameter rhythms and romantic story made it popular in primary school classrooms. It was even used explicitly to teach reading in the 1898 textbook *The Hiawatha Primer*, which uses Longfellow's poem to teach children to read through "pedagogical repetition of words and phrases" (Compton-Lilly et al. 291). This primer is a good example of whole-language reading instruction from more than a century ago and would have competed with the Dick and Jane Basic Readers. As a common text in schools, Longfellow's poem helped to create a shared sense of American identity, but as a cultural record it is a problematic whitewashing of American history and homogenized representation of American Indian cultures.

Published just two decades after the passing of the Indian Removal Act (1831) and the forced removal of the Cherokee from Georgia (1839), and amid debates about slavery and abolitionism, *The Song of Hiawatha* presented a unified American origin story at a time when Americans could not agree on shared values. In doing so, however, it helped to inscribe the Romantic trope of the "vanishing Indian" indelibly onto American consciousness. Tom Nurmi argues that the poem "is a retrograde prophecy. Its action begins in the mythic fog of pre-national lore, yet the way it articulates an 'original' cultural encounter echoes a variety of ongoing conflicts in midcentury America" (245). The trope of the vanishing Indian was common in the decades of and directly after the passing of the Indian Removal Act, with poets such as William Cullen Bryant writing about the inevitable westward expansion of white settlers and the disappearance of indigenous peoples. The speaker of Bryant's 1832 poem "The Prairies," for example, imagines an "advancing multitude" of "Sabbath worshippers" that will replace the "warlike and fierce … red man," who "Has left the blooming wilds he ranged so long" (lines 116, 120, 58–59, 90). Longfellow makes this misleading trope a central plot point of *Hiawatha*, thus embedding it into America's origin story.

Hiawatha's departure "To the land of Hereafter" (206) at the end of the poem is a fitting, grand exit for the hero of an epic, but it also romanticizes the removal of American Indian peoples from their homelands and their assimilation into Christianity. Before leaving, for example, Hiawatha "Turned and waved his hand at parting," and then "Westward, westward Hiawatha / Sailed into the fiery sunset, / Sailed into the purple vapors, / Sailed into the dusk of evening" (205). The Romantic imagery here heightens the emotional climax and the finality of Hiawatha's leaving, as the people on the shore say, "'Farewell for ever!' / Said, 'Farewell, O Hiawatha!'" (205). Hiawatha is replaced by Christianity in his people's esteem, telling them to welcome the white, Christian newcomers. "I have seen it in a vision," he says, "Seen the great canoe with pinions, / Seen the people with white faces, / Seen the coming of this bearded / People of the wooden vessel" (196). Their coming is ordained by "Gitche Manito the Mighty / The Great Spirit, the Creator," who "Sends them hither on his errand, / Sends them to us with his message" (196). And, in fact, when "the Black-Robe chief, the Pale-face, / With the cross upon his bosom, / Landed on the sandy margin," Hiawatha welcomes him with open arms, crying,

> Beautiful is the sun, O strangers,
> When you come so far to see us!
> All our town in peace awaits you,
> All our doors stand open for you;
> You shall enter all our wigwams,
> For the heart's right hand we give you. (200)

While readers in the 1850s may have appreciated a peaceful cultural encounter between different peoples, *Hiawatha* brings this about by ignoring the forced relocation of American Indian nations. The present tense used to describe the entrance of the white Christian missionaries contrasts with the past tense used to describe Hiawatha's departure, for example. The present is white and Christian, whereas the past is Indian.

Longfellow's poem also inscribes the nineteenth-century idea of Manifest Destiny, suggesting that American westward expansion was inevitable. Just like the speaker of Bryant's poem "The Prairies," Hiawatha has a vision in which he sees white settlers expanding across the continent. He

> behold[s] the westward marches
> Of the unknown, crowded nations.
> All the land was full of people,
> Restless, struggling, toiling, striving,
> Speaking many tongues, yet feeling
> But one heart-beat in their bosoms. (197)

Readers know the people in this prosperous vision do not include American Indians because Hiawatha clarifies, "I beheld our nations scattered, / All forgetful of my counsels, / Weakened, warring with each other" (197). The implication here is not only that there is no place for American Indians in the future Hiawatha sees, but also that American Indians are to blame for it. Further, because the visions experienced by the speaker of Bryant's poem and by Hiawatha in Longfellow's poem are described in transcendentalist terms, they are presented as received spiritual knowledge rather than historical fantasy.

Scholarly debates about *The Song of Hiawatha* address multiple levels of cultural pastiche, obfuscation, and silencing in regard to Longfellow's source materials. For example, many debates focus on claims that Longfellow plagiarized from the Finnish epic the *Kalevala* and from the writings of Henry Rowe Schoolcraft, a geographer and Indian Agent who lived in what is now Michigan (Osborn and Osborn ix). Other scholars, such as Stith Thompson, point out many inaccuracies about Indian folklore borrowed from Schoolcraft, such as his assertion that "Manabozho, the demigod of Ojibwa and their Algonquian kinsmen, is identical with the Iroquois Hiawatha," even though "there is not a point of resemblance between them" (129). Thompson notes that "Hiawatha … was an historical character, an Iroquois statesman of the Mohawk tribe" and not the character we see in Longfellow's poem (130). Scholarly consensus is that *Hiawatha* does not present an accurate representation of American Indian myth or American history. More recently, scholars have argued that the real source for Longfellow's poem and Schoolcraft's writing was actually Schoolcraft's wife, Jane Johnston Schoolcraft, also known by her Ojibwe name, Bamewawage-zhikaquay (Parker). Thus, in addition to attributing white assumptions of Manifest Destiny to a historically inaccurate Indian hero, the poem ignores the cultural complexity of Indian nations and the contributions of an actual Ojibwe author.

The Hiawatha Primer, published by Florence Holbrook in 1898, is designed to help young readers learn to read through whole-language methods. Holbrook's advice in a section called "Suggestions to Teachers" sounds remarkably similar to the whole-language movement of the 1980s and 1990s. "[P]honics, word and sentence drills are excluded from the text," she writes, and the primer uses a set list of words in increasingly complex sentences so that the "initial sentences will at first be recognized and discriminated by the child as wholes only" (I). Holbrook also advocates reading words in context, because "the child will master new word forms much more easily if they are presented to him in their natural thought relations," that is, not in decontextualized lists of words (I). Indeed, the first chapter begins with the sentences "Hiawatha was an Indian boy. / Nokomis was his grandmother" (1) and eventually leads up to an excerpt from Longfellow's poem:

> By the shores of Gitche Gumee,
> By the shining Big-Sea-Water,
> Stood the wigwam of Nokomis.
> Dark behind it rose the forest,
> Rose the black and gloomy pine-trees,
> Rose the first with cones upon them;
> Bright before it beat the water,
> Beat the clear and sunny water,
> Beat the shining Big-Sea Water. (14)

The *Primer* focuses on Hiawatha's childhood, presumably to appeal to child readers, and does not include the overt themes of Manifest Destiny present in the full poem. However, through constant repetition of sentences, words, and illustrations, the *Primer* presents a generic portrait of American Indian cultures and an "Indian boy" with a Romantic (i.e., ahistorical) connection to nature and wild animals. While the Dick and Jane Basic Readers reinforce white US culture's view of itself, *The Hiawatha Primer* reinforces white US culture's view of American Indians. And Holbrook's dedication "[t]o the many children who have yet to unlock the storehouse of the world's great literature" suggests that the purpose of the *Primer* is ultimately to get children to read Longfellow's full poem (iii).

So many generations of school children read and memorized sections of *Hiawatha* (either Holbrook's *Primer* or Longfellow's original poem) that it became embedded in American culture and memory in surprising ways. Even though it was published in 1855, the poem continued to be popular well into the twentieth century. Popular cartoons, for example, included Disney's Silly Symphony *Little Hiawatha* (1937), Warner Brothers' *Hiawatha's Rabbit Hunt* (1941), and Tex Avery's *Big Heel-watha* (1944). A joke involving characters spontaneously reciting lines from *The Song of Hiawatha* runs through popular culture throughout the twentieth century and into the twenty-first, further suggesting the ubiquity of the poem in the American consciousness. Examples include the 1947 RKO film *Magic Town*, the 1957 20th Century-Fox film *Desk Set*, an episode of the 1979 television show *Carol Burnett & Company* ("Carl's Grave"), and a 2006 episode of *The Simpsons* ("Million Dollar Abie"). I have no idea how many times this joke has been made in American popular culture, but it would not work unless the writers could count on their audiences being familiar with the poem.

The Song of Hiawatha has had considerable cultural reach because of its presence in American schools. Nurmi argues that "Hiawatha's popularity reflects the desire of American readers to rehearse a coherent narrative of U.S. history, even—and perhaps especially—when they acknowledge its inconsistencies or outright revisionary content" (244). *Hiawatha* represents the difficulty of identifying a cohesive national identity without revisionist silences of marginalized groups. *The Hiawatha Primer* reinscribes those historical silences, embedding them into American literacy itself by asking early readers to rehearse these silences repeatedly (just as the Dick and Jane Basic Readers do). In fact, in their study of American reading textbooks, Compton-Lilly and colleagues found, "Many [early twentieth-century] US textbooks reflect and reinforce existing biases and stereotypes about Native American people while ignoring historical oppression and violence…. Native people are treated as a singular group silencing the richness and complexity of native tribes, languages, cultures and lives" (291–92). The historical silences in the text are political, even if well-intentioned.

Unlike book challengers, however, I do not think Longfellow's poem or Holbrook's *Primer* should be banned from classrooms and school libraries just because they do not conform to my worldview. The poem is a cultural fantasy that perpetuates harmful stereotypes, but there are nevertheless good reasons to teach *Hiawatha* today—to deconstruct the trope of the vanishing Indian, for example. The culturally responsible way to do so is to teach the context, as well. When I teach it, I also assign texts by American Indian authors, such as Ojibwe poet Jane Johnston Schoolcraft's poetry (published in 2007 in a collection called *The Sound the Stars Make Rushing*

Through the Sky), Pequot minister William Apess's 1831 autobiography *A Son of the Forest* and 1836 speech "Eulogy of King Philip," the 1833 *Life of Ma-ka-tai-me-she-kia-kiak or Black Hawk* (a Sauk chief), and Cherokee editor Elias Boudinot's editorials in *The Cherokee Phoenix*. While they do not agree with each other, each of these writers addresses the clash of American and indigenous cultures in the early nineteenth century without relying on the Romantic trope of the vanishing Indian and without flattening Indian nations into one stereotype. In other words, they provide narratives of American history that encourage students to think critically and grapple with complexity and cognitive dissonance.

Advice for English and Language Arts Teachers

If you teach reading or literature, you are a cultural gatekeeper. There is no getting around that. Educators are not the only gatekeepers of books—librarians, parents, publishers, literary agents, prize committees, book reviewers, book sellers, scholars, and a whole host of other people affect whether and how a book gets to readers—but gatekeeping is the reality of an educational system in which students are told what to read. That is true at any level of education in the United States (and most countries in the world) from kindergarten to postgraduate study. And, in fact, most American high schools assign American literature to teach students about American history and values. The recent rise in book challenges and classical charter schools and the recent popularity of the "science of reading" may suggest that teaching reading and literature can somehow be apolitical, that we can somehow avoid all the ideological stuff, but that is not the case. Literature is not written or read in a cultural vacuum, and educators must make reading decisions that have political implications. Thus, this essay is a long-winded way to argue that English and Languages Arts educators do not have the luxury of avoiding political subjects. Reading and literacy are political.

The recent trend of challenging books is based in large part on radical de-contextualization of literature, both reading excerpts out of context and trying to avoid books that challenge homogeneous views of American history and portray the historical and contemporary realities of marginalized people. The best way to resist that is to insist on contextualizing literature—its use in the classroom, its engagement with historical/cultural ideas, and as whole texts. I am not suggesting that educators promote a particular ideological worldview but that they articulate why they have assigned literary texts. The course syllabus and/or assignment prompts should explain the reasons for and contexts in which students will be engaging with the assigned literature.

Following is my advice to educators who are worried about book challenges.

Articulate Why You Are Assigning Literature

Teaching is an act of communication, and it is important for every teacher to understand the rhetorical situation of that communication. Who are you as a teacher? Who are your students? What is your purpose in assigning literature in the classroom? What are the methods of instruction you will use to achieve this communication? What is the context (personal and professional) you bring to the classroom? What contexts affect your students' learning? Contemporary educational training encourages this understanding of your rhetorical situation through a variety of professional practices you can use to contextualize the use of literature in the classroom.

Know what learning outcomes you are trying to achieve. Employing backward design for your courses will help clarify the purpose of assigning literary texts. That means starting with learning outcomes. What are the learning outcomes mandated by your state, district, or program? What are the outcomes you think students should learn? There are many reasons to assign literary texts: improving reading comprehension and critical thinking; learning to pay attention to detail; learning about a particular place, time period, or culture; analyzing models for the students' own writing; practicing critical thinking by applying different critical lenses; practicing and assessing information literacy; getting students excited about reading; etc. Know your purpose(s) in assigning literature.

Articulate your pedagogical methods. There are many ways to achieve learning outcomes, but knowing what your outcomes are will help to clarify what pedagogical methods will best achieve them. High-impact practices, for example, target multiple outcomes at once. Problem-based methods encourage active learning because students must teach themselves skills and knowledge to achieve their project goals. Scaffolded pedagogies walk students through a series of skills to complete a complicated product (such as a research essay). Equity-minded practices recognize and try to remove educational barriers students experience. Your pedagogical methods should align with course outcomes.

Determine who is responsible for choosing what students will read. Choosing literary texts for a class involves answering a series of questions, some of which you may not have control over. Do you (or the school) choose the texts or do you let students choose what they will read? If you choose the texts, will you focus on canonical texts, non-canonical texts, or a combination of both? If the students choose their own texts, will you limit their choices? Will you assign a basal reader (like a literature anthology) or whole texts? What is your budget for textbooks? Do students have access to electronic devices and/or the Internet to access OER materials? Knowing the learning outcomes and pedagogical methods you will use can help to answer these questions.

Be intentional about how you are contextualizing the assigned literary texts for your students. Regardless of the exact methods of reading instruction, we know that knowledge-building is important for reading comprehension. There are many contexts that can help readers make meaning of texts: literary context, historical context, national context, cultural context, etc. A Language Arts educator should teach students to read in all these contexts, but not necessarily all of them at the same time. To understand modernism, for example, readers need to understand not just what modernism is but what it is reacting against. To understand free verse, readers need to know something about poetic form. To understand the significance of the Dick and Jane Basic Readers in *The Bluest Eye*, students may need to learn about the book's many references to 1930s and 1940s American popular culture. To understand why *The Song of Hiawatha* perpetuates harmful stereotypes of American Indians, students may need to learn about American Indian writers of the time.

Give book challenges full consideration. Because literacy is inherently ideological, all educators should regularly interrogate their choices in the classroom. *The Song of Hiawatha* was a beloved classroom staple for much of the nineteenth and twentieth centuries, but many people today see it as culturally harmful. It is okay to reassess literary texts and your reasons for assigning them in the classroom. That does not mean you should give in to every book challenge, but you should be willing to listen to challenges and articulate your reasons for assigning a book.

Know the Policies That Apply to Your Classroom

Most schools already have in place policies about the selection of texts in classes and school libraries. It is a good idea to know what those policies are before your classes begin. Many state and school district policies are in flux right now with the introduction of Parents Rights bills in many states, but when districts and individual educators are faced with a book challenge, policies guide the process and help to create a template for discussions.

The Challenged Materials Committee of the Rockwood School District in Eureka, Missouri, for example, released a committee report in December 2021 about a challenge to the graphic novel *Gender Queer* by Maia Kobabe that provides a good template for considering challenges. The Committee's review was thorough and includes sections on (1) regulations governing the Committee, (2) policies from the district's library media handbook, (3) professional reviews & awards regarding this material, (4) concerns the challenger brought about the book (i.e., that four images in the book are pornographic and therefore illegal according to Missouri code), (5) the Missouri code that defines pornographic content for minors, (6) the Committee's comments about the value of the book, and (7) the Committee's rationale and decision (Challenged Materials Committee). This is a good template to follow when addressing a challenge. By following the district's policies, the Committee decided to retain the book without restriction (Challenged Materials Committee). Upon appeal of this decision, the Appeals Committee of the Board of Education upheld the Committee's decision in February 2022 (Appeals Committee).

In today's climate, policies and legislation may change rapidly. Upon the passing of SB775 by the Missouri legislature in August 2022 (which I discuss in the next section), for example, *Gender Queer* was removed from Rockwood School District libraries after all ("Response to Library Legislation"). Even though policies may change, however, they articulate on the institutional level the reasons for assigning or making books available to students and should therefore be the framework by which book challenges are assessed.

Know the Laws That Apply to Your Classroom
The more difficult concern right now is legislation passed by states that is vague, misleading, nonsensical, or discriminatory. Recent Parents Rights legislation passed in Iowa in July 2023, SF 496, for example, caused panic among some Iowa school districts. The same legislation that prohibits gender-affirming care for minors (§ 24) also mandates that school libraries may contain only "age-appropriate" materials (§ 2) that "[do] not include any material with descriptions or visual depictions of a sex act" (§ 4); and that a "school district shall not provide any program, curriculum, test, survey, questionnaire, promotion, or instruction relating to gender identity or sexual orientation to students in kindergarten through grade six" (§ 16).

Because the new legislation calls for disciplinary action against any school district employee found violating these new laws, some districts in the state have taken drastic measures to comply. The Assistant Superintendent of the Mason City Community School District, for example, turned to generative AI, ChatGPT, to determine whether individual books "describe a sex act" and accidentally ignited a national debate when books like Buzz Bissenger's 1990 non-fiction book *Friday Night Lights* were identified as inappropriate. The debate centered around the fact that ChatGPT was inaccurate in identifying whether a book contains descriptions of a sex act (Hernandez). The real conversation, however, should be that the law is difficult to interpret. When defining the phrase "age-appropriate" for library materials, for example, SF 496 specifies, "For the purposes of this section, '*Age-appropriate*' means topics, messages, and teaching methods suitable to particular ages or groups of children and adolescents, based on developing cognitive, emotional, and behavioral capacity typical for the age or group. 'Age appropriate' does not include any material with descriptions or visual depictions of a sex act as defined in section 702.17" (§ 4). The definition of "sex act" in Section 702.17 of Iowa Code, is really specific, though. The code states,

The term "sex act" or "sexual activity" means any sexual contact between two or more persons by any of the following:

1. Penetration of the penis into the vagina or anus.
2. Contact between mouth and genitalia or mouth and anus or by contact between the genitalia of one person and the genitalia or anus of another person.
3. Contact between the finger, hand, or other body part of one person and the genitalia or anus of another person, except in the course of examination or treatment by a person licensed pursuant to chapter 148, 148c, 151, or 152.
4. Ejaculation onto the person of another.
5. By use of artificial sexual organs or substitutes thereof in contact with the genitalia or anus.
6. The touching of a person's own genitals or anus with a finger, hand, or artificial sexual organ or other similar device at the direction of another person. (§ 702.17)

This definition would not apply to nakedness, masturbation (unless at the direction of another person), non-explicit descriptions of sex, mention of sex toys, etc. It would not even apply to a description or visual depiction of two characters having sex unless there was explicit mention or depiction of one person having contact with the genitals of another person. Removal of a book from school libraries would therefore likely be dependent on the vague phrase "based on developing cognitive, emotional, and behavioral capacity typical for the age or group." Who determines the cognitive, emotional, or behavioral capacity of a child "typical for the age or group" is not clarified.

Iowa Code's definitions of "gender identity" and "sexual orientation" create similar problems for interpretation. Section 16 of SF 496 creates a new law (§ 279.80 Sexual orientation and gender identity - prohibited instruction). The text reads,

1. As used in this section:

"Gender identity" means the same as defined in section 216.2.

"Sexual orientation" means the same as defined in section 216.2. A school district shall not provide any program, curriculum, test, survey, questionnaire, promotion, or instruction relating to gender identity or sexual orientation to students in kindergarten through grade six. (§ 16)

However, Section 216.2 of Iowa Code specifies that "'*Gender identity*' means a gender-related identity of a person, regardless of the person's assigned sex at birth" and "'*Sexual orientation*' means actual or perceived heterosexuality, homosexuality, or bisexuality." The law clearly intends to prohibit instruction about queer gender identities and sexualities, but it could be read to mean that educators cannot give any materials to students in kindergarten through grade six that mention any gender identity or "perceived heterosexuality, homosexuality, or bisexuality." So, no math problems involving boys or girls or people with gender-specific names? Or books that include mommies and daddies? I do not see how this new law could be enforced.

Missouri's SB775, which is a bill about child sexual abuse and exploitation passed in August 2022, criminalizes visual sexual content of any kind in schools, making it a class A misdemeanor. The bill creates a new section of Missouri Code, Section 573.550, which reads,

1. A person commits the offense of providing explicit sexual material to a student if such person is affiliated with a public or private elementary or secondary school in an official capacity and, knowing of its content and character, such person provides, assigns, supplies, distributes, loans, or coerces acceptance of or the approval of the providing of explicit sexual material to a student or possesses with the purpose of providing, assigning, supplying, distributing, loaning, or coercing acceptance of or the approval of the providing of explicit sexual material to a student.
…
(1) "Explicit sexual material", any pictorial, three-dimensional, or visual depiction, including any photography, film, video, picture, or computer-generated image, showing human masturbation, deviate sexual intercourse

as defined in section 566.010, sexual intercourse, direct physical stimulation of genitals, sadomasochistic abuse, or emphasizing the depiction of postpubertal human genitals; provided, however, that works of art, when taken as a whole, that have serious artistic significance, or works of anthropological significance, or materials used in science courses, including but not limited to materials used in biology, anatomy, physiology, and sexual education classes shall not be deemed to be within the foregoing definition;

This definition of "explicit sexual material" manages to be both sweeping and vague at the same time. Although the definition makes exception for "works of art, when taken as a whole, that have serious artistic significance" (i.e., works of art considered in context), what counts as "explicit sexual material" includes much more than Iowa's prohibition of depictions of sexual acts. In Missouri's law, even depicting adult human genitals is criminalized. PEN America has compiled a list of almost 300 books that were removed from school libraries as a result of this new law. Titles include graphic novels with queer characters, multiple art and art history books, and several books about the Holocaust ("Missouri Book Bans"). I do not think this was the intent of SB775, but it was the result.

The biggest outcome of these recent laws in Iowa and Missouri seems to be confusion. These laws may be successful in making educators fear criminal prosecution for teaching, but they do not clarify what books contradict the current political mood in each state legislature.

Conclusion

The involvement of state legislatures in recent book challenges has introduced multiple complications to the already complex choices English and Language Arts educators face when assigning literature. It may be years before these vague and confusing new laws are sorted out. However, educators can navigate this moment by making intentional pedagogical choices about the texts they teach, following established policies for their district and school, and insisting that literature be read in context.

Hastings College

Works Cited

Altwerger, Bess, et al. "Whole Language: What's New?" *The Reading Teacher*, vol. 41, no. 2, Nov. 1987, pp. 144–54. *JSTOR*.

Androne, Helane Adams. "Introduction: Teaching to the (Con)Text." *Multiethnic American Literatures: Essays for Teaching Context and Culture*, edited by Helane Adams Androne, McFarland, 2015.

Appeals Committee of the Board of Education. "Board of Education Appeal Process Reporting Form - Gender Queer, by Maia Kobabe." *Rockwood School District* [Eureka, Missouri], 17 Feb. 2022, www.rsdmo.org/Page/6736.

"Book Ban Data." *American Library Association*, 2023, www.ala.org/advocacy/bbooks/book-ban-data.

Bryant, William Cullen. "The Prairies." *The Poetry Foundation*, www.poetryfoundation.org/poems/55341/the-prairies.

Challenged Materials Committee, "Challenged Materials Committee Report - Gender Queer, by Maia Kobabe." *Rockwood School District* [Eureka, Missouri], 6 Dec. 2021, www.rsdmo.org/Page/6736.

Compton-Lilly, Catherine, et al. "A Problematic Legacy: Diversity in American Reading Textbooks." *Journal for Multicultural Education*, vol. 13, no. 4, 2019, pp. 289–301.

DiMarco, Bella. "Legislative Tracker: 2022 Parents-Rights Bills in the States." *Future Ed*, 6 June 2022, www.future-ed.org/legislative-tracker-parent-rights-bills-in-the-states/.

———. "Legislative Tracker: 2023 Parents-Rights Bills in the States." *Future Ed*, 16 Mar. 2023, www.future-ed.org/legislative-tracker-2023-parent-rights-bills-in-the-states/.

DuBois, W. E. B. *The Souls of Black Folk: Essays and Sketches*. A. C. McClurg & Co., 1903.

Garcia, Raymond. "Book Challenges Nearly Doubled from 2021." *American Library Association*, 22 Mar. 2022, www.ala.org/news/press-releases/2023/03/record-book-bans-2022. Press release.

Hernandez, Samantha. "An Iowa School Official Needed to Know If 42 Books Contained Sex. She Asked ChatGPT for Help." *Des Moines Register*, 16 Aug. 2023, www.desmoinesregister.com/story/news/education/2023/08/16/iowa-school-district-uses-chatgpt-ai-to-answer-if-41-books-have-sex-acts/70598610007/.

"High School Reading List." *Great Hearts*, www.greatheartsamerica.org/great-hearts-life/great-hearts-curriculum/high-school-reading/.

Holbrook, Florence. *The Hiawatha Primer.* Houghton, Mifflin and Company, 1898.

"Home." *Great Hearts*, www.greatheartsamerica.org/.

"Integrated Humanities Program Reading List (9-12)." *Valor Education*, www.valoreducation.org/reading-lists.

Iowa State, Legislature. Iowa Code §216.2 Definitions. *Iowa State Legislature*, www.legis.iowa.gov/docs/code/216.2.pdf.

———, ———. Iowa Code §702.17 Sex Act. *Iowa State Legislature*, www.legis.iowa.gov/docs/ico/section/702.17.pdf.

———, ———. Senate File 496. *Iowa State Legislature*, 26 May 2023, www.legis.iowa.gov/docs/publications/LGE/90/SF496.pdf.

"Literacies and Languages for All: Focusing on Whole Language as a Dynamic Philosophy of Education." *National Council of Teachers of English*, ncte.org/groups/lla/.

Longfellow, Henry Wadsworth. *The Song of Hiawatha.* 1855. Henry Altemus, 1898.

Martinez, Miriam G. and Lea M. McGee. "Children's Literature and Reading Instruction: Past, Present, and Future." *Reading Research Quarterly*, vol. 35, no. 1, Mar. 2000, pp. 154–69. *JSTOR*.

Meehan, Kasey, et al. "Banned in the USA: The Mounting Pressure to Censor." *PEN America*, 2023, pen.org/report/book-bans-pressure-to-censor.

"Missouri Book Bans in Response to SB 775 - 2022." Spreadsheet, *PEN America*, docs.google.com/spreadsheets/d/1AVW8q-B4uSZIJ3mLqc5tY8DZyojI1KLIVBQzSCb7lbg/edit#gid=0. Google document.

Missouri State, Legislature. Missouri Code Senate Bill 775. *Missouri State Legislature*, 30 June 2022, www.senate.mo.gov/22info/pdf-bill/tat/SB775.pdf.

Morrison, Toni. *The Bluest Eye*. 1970. Plume, 1994.

Natanson, Hannah. "Objection to Sexual, LGBTQ Content Propels Spike in Book Challenges." *The Washington Post*, 23 May 2023, www.washingtonpost.com/education/2023/05/23/lgbtq-book-ban-challengers/.

Nurmi, Tom. "Writing Ojibwe: Politics and Poetics in Longfellow's Hiawatha." *The Journal of American Culture*, vol. 35, no. 3, Sept. 2012, pp. 244–57.

"100 Most Frequently Challenged Books: 1990-1999." *American Library Association*, www.ala.org/advocacy/bbooks/frequentlychallengedbooks/decade1999

"100 Most Frequently Challenged Books: 2000-2009." *American Library Association*, www.ala.org/advocacy/bbooks/frequentlychallengedbooks/decade2009

"100 Most Frequently Challenged Books: 2010-2019." *American Library Association*, www.ala.org/advocacy/bbooks/frequentlychallengedbooks/decade2019

Osborn, Chase S. and Stellanova Osborn. *Schoolcraft > Longfellow > Hiawatha*. The Jacques Cattell Press, 1942.

Parker, Robert Dale. "Introduction." *The Sound the Stars Make Rushing Through the Sky: The Writings of Jane Johnston Schoolcraft,* by Jane Johnston Schoolcraft. U of Pennsylvania P, 2008.

"Response to Library Legislation." *Rockwood School District* [Eureka, Missouri], www.rsdmo.org/Page/6867.

Schreiber, Evelyn Jaffe. "Double Consciousness." *Toni Morrison's* The Bluest Eye, edited by Harold Bloom, 2010, pp. 82–87. Bloom's Literary Criticism.

Schwartz, Sarah. "With Moms for Liberty Endorsement, 'Science of Reading' Faces More Political Controversy." *Education Week*, 9 Oct.2023, www.edweek.org/teaching-learning/with-moms-for-liberty-endorsement-science-of-reading-faces-more-political-controversy/2023/10.

Thompson, Stith. "The Indian Legend of Hiawatha." *PMLA*, vol. 37, no. 1, Mar. 1922, pp. 128–40.

"Top 13 Most Challenged Books of 2022." *American Library Association*, www.ala.org/advocacy/bbooks/frequentlychallengedbooks/top10.

"We Are Winning Because of YOU!" *Moms for Liberty*, www.momsforliberty.org/about/. Video.

Werrlein, Debra T. "Not So Fast, Dick and Jane: Reimagining Childhood and Nation in *The Bluest Eye*." *MELUS*, vol. 30, No. 4, winter 2005, pp. 53–72.

"Who We Are." *Moms for Liberty*, www.momsforliberty.org/about/.

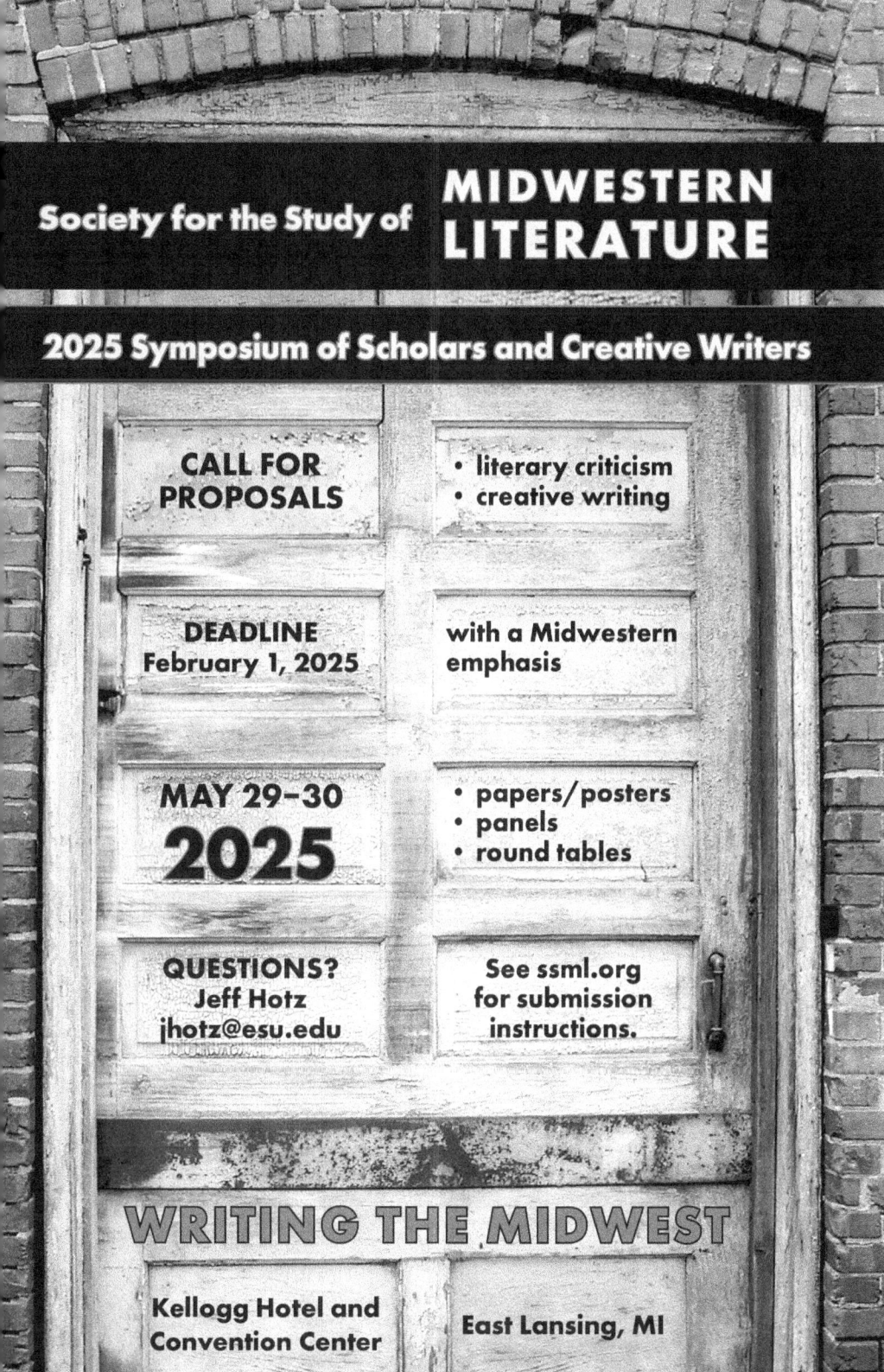

Society for the Study of **MIDWESTERN LITERATURE**

2025 Symposium of Scholars and Creative Writers

CALL FOR PROPOSALS

- literary criticism
- creative writing

DEADLINE
February 1, 2025

with a Midwestern emphasis

MAY 29–30
2025

- papers/posters
- panels
- round tables

QUESTIONS?
Jeff Hotz
jhotz@esu.edu

See ssml.org for submission instructions.

WRITING THE MIDWEST

Kellogg Hotel and Convention Center

East Lansing, MI

CALL FOR PROPOSALS

1925 was a banner year for Midwestern literature. Important novels published that year include F. Scott Fitzgerald's *The Great Gatsby*, Willa Cather's *The Professor's House*, Ernest Hemingway's *In Our Time*, Theodore Dreiser's *An American Tragedy*, and Sinclair Lewis's *Arrowsmith*. To celebrate the 100th anniversary of this important year, the Society for the Study of Midwestern Literature invites essay proposals for a special issue of its peer-reviewed journal *Midwestern Miscellany* on the topic of "Midwestern Literature in 1925," to be edited by Scott Emmert (University of Wisconsin Oshkosh). Proposals may focus on the famous novels of 1925 or texts / authors that have been overshadowed by Fitzgerald, Cather, Hemingway, Dreiser, and Lewis.

Proposals should be no more than 300 words and should include a brief critical bibliography. Completed essays should be between 3,000 and 5,000 words. Contributors must be members of SSML before publication.

PROPOSAL DEADLINE	ESSAY DEADLINE
January 1, 2025	August 1, 2025

Send proposal and short CV to Scott Emmert (emmerts@uwosh.edu). Please also indicate if you would like your proposal to be considered for a special panel at the 2025 Symposium of the Society for the Study of Midwestern Literature (May 29-30, East Lansing, MI).

NEED SOME INSPIRATION? LESSER KNOWN TEXTS PUBLISHED IN 1925

Bess Streeter Aldrich, *The Rim of the Prairie*
Sherwood Anderson, *Dark Laughter*
Lorna Doone Beers, *Prairie Fires*
Earl Derr Biggers, *The House Without a Key*
Thomas A. Boyd, *Samuel Drummond*
Louis Bromfield, *Possession*
Hallie Quinn Brown, *Tales My Father Told*
Edgar Rice Burroughs, *The Moon Men*
Edgar Rice Burroughs, *The Red Hawk*
Floyd Dell, *This Mad Ideal* and *Runaway*
John Dos Passos, *Manhattan Transfer*
Geoffrey Dell Eaton, *Backfurrow*
T. S. Eliot, "The Hollow Men"
John T. Frederick, *Green Bush*
Ruth Gaines-Shelton, "The Church Fight"
Zane Grey, *The Vanishing American*
John Herrmann, *Foreign Born*

Emerson Hough, *The Ship of Souls*
Langston Hughes, "The Weary Blues"
Alain Locke (ed.), *The New Negro*
Archibald Macleish, *The Pot of Earth*
Walter J. Mullenburg, *Prairie*
Martha Ostenso, *Wild Geese*
O.E. Rolvaag, *Giants in the Earth*
Helen Hooven Santmyer, *Herbs and Apples*
James Stevens, *Paul Bunyan*
Gene Stratton-Porter, *The Keeper of the Bees*
Ruth Suckow, *The Odyssey of a Nice Girl*
Ruth Plumly Thompson, *The Lost King of Oz*
Jim Tully, *Jarnegan*
Carl Van Vechten, *Firecrackers: A Realistic Novel*
Glenway Wescott, *Natives of Rock*
Harold Bell Wright, *A Son of the Father*
Little magazines: *Poetry*, *The Midland*, etc.

www.ingramcontent.com/pod-product-compliance
Lightning Source LLC
Chambersburg PA
CBHW070749120626
46557CB00002B/510